UNDERSTANDING EXECUTIVE STRESS

CARY L. COOPER
and
JUDI MARSHALL

PBI
a petrocelli
book
new york / princeton

First printed and published in the United States by PBI Books

1 2 3 4 5 6 7 8 9 10

Library of Congress Cataloging in Publication Data

Cooper, Cary L
  Understanding executive stress.

  "A Petrocelli book."
  Bibliography: p.
  Includes index.
  1. Executives. 2. Stress (Physiology)
3. Executives—Psychology. I. Marshall, Judi, joint
author. II. Title.
HF5500.2.C56   658.4'001'9   77–16077
ISBN 0–89433–059–4

This volume is dedicated to our social support team:
Richie, June, Scott, Beth and Pat

CONTENTS

54- 79

120- 1415

ACKNOWLEDGMENTS

We should like to thank the following journals and publishers for allowing us to draw on articles written by the authors in preparing this book.

Journal of Occupational Psychology and the British Psychological Society

Management Decision and *M.C.B. Publications*

Management International Review and the *European Foundation for Management Development*

Personnel Review and *Gower Press*

INTRODUCTION

The main aim of this book is to provide the reader with a better understanding of the sources of stress acting upon managers in organizations. We have drawn on a wide range of sources for our material—from novels to research reports, from writers concerned with organizational effectiveness to those whose aim is to improve the quality of working life. In so doing we have not, however, been satisfied just to review the literature, but have chosen to tie it to an underlying model, that of Person : Environment fit, and to elaborate underlying conceptual implications as this seems appropriate.

Chapters 1 and 2 are intended to give the reader a broad grounding in the topic area via an examination of various ways in which stress can be defined and a review of some of the available literature. In chapter 3 the Person : Environment fit model is applied specifically to managerial stress and potential sources of stress in both the immediate job environment and "in" the individual are considered. Building on this, a wider view of the manager is then taken and the pressures which may result from working in an organization, with other organizational members, are discussed. Our view of the manager is finally expanded one step further to consider possible problems at the interface between his work and home life. Particular attention is paid to the meaning for their joint lives of the role his wife adopts. Having built up a static picture of the manager and his wife, we then conclude the description of potential stressors by considering the importance of timing in the stress sequence and illustrate some of its facets by following the couple through a potentially stressful event—relocation.

This extensive consideration of stressors provides a sound base from which to suggest ways that both organizations and individuals can cope more effectively. Chapter 7 does just this, but emphasizes that as pressures have beneficial as well as destructive effects, stress must be *managed* rather than totally eradicated. In the first half, three broad strategies are proposed—prevention, the remedying of known common environmental stressors and the provision of means to handle stress once it has occurred. The second half considers the role the personnel officer might play in this context.

In the final chapter we point to some of the shortcomings of current research methodology in this area and make suggestions for future studies.

Before proceeding, a short explanatory note: In this time of increasingly vocal concern for equal opportunities, the fact that this book concentrates on the *male manager* and his female spouse requires, perhaps, some justification. We do not mean by this bias to suggest that managers should be male but to reflect the status quo, that the overwhelming majority are male. In consequence, there is little or no research work dealing with the stresses on female managers. We feel, therefore, that it is more worthwhile, for the present, to focus on topics which have been explored than to speculate about those which are a future research need.

1
WHAT IS STRESS?

The Principles of Newspeak:
"The purpose of Newspeak was not only to provide a medium of expression for the world-view and
mental habits proper to the devotees of Ingsoc, but to
make all other modes of thought impossible. It was
intended that when Newspeak had been adopted
once and for all and Oldspeak forgotten, a heretical
thought—that is, a thought diverging from the principles of Ingsoc—should be literally unthinkable, at
least as far as thought is dependent on words. . . .
Newspeak was designed not to extend but to *dimish*
the range of thought, and this purpose was indirectly
assisted by cutting the choice of words down to a
minimum."

Orwell (1949)

Big Brother appreciated, and used to advantage, the
intimate relationship between language and thought. In
understanding the meaning of a theoretical concept, it is

often instructive to explore its use both over time and simultaneously in different contexts. This approach will be adopted here; four complementary perspectives will be taken. The historical development of the term stress will first be described; it will then be defined operationally in terms of its cost to the individual concerned and to the national economy.

STRESS: A BRIEF HISTORY OF THE TERM

Stress (a word derived from Latin) was used popularly in the seventeenth century to mean "hardship, straits, adversity or affliction." Only during the eighteenth and nineteenth centuries did its use evolve to denote "force, pressure, strain or strong effort" with reference now also to objects but still primarily to a person or a person's "organs or mental powers" (Hinkle, 1973). It was these connotations of an external pressure being resisted by the person/object which it sought to distort and disrupt which were taken up when the term gained currency in engineering and physics (and which have subsequently been passed on to social scientists). Although the concept was apparently employed by Boyle (investigating the properties of gases) and Hooke (elasticity of springs) in the seventeenth century, Hinkle (1973) credits its earliest precise definition to Baron Cauchy (Love, 1944) in the early nineteenth century. In physics, then, "stress" refers to the internal force generated within a solid body by the action of any external force which tends to distort the body; "strain" is the resulting distortion and the external force producing the distortion is called "load" (Figure 1.1).

Figure 1.1

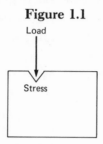

The idea that "stress and strain" contribute to long-term ill health (rather than merely short-term discomfort implicit in the above definition) can be found early on in the concept's development. In 1910, for example, Sir William Osler noted that angina pectoris was especially common among the Jewish members of the business community and attributed this, in part, to their hectic pace of life: "Living an intense life, absorbed in his work, devoted to his pleasures, passionately devoted to his home, the nervous energy of the Jew is taxed to the uttermost, and his system is subjected to that stress and strain which seems to be a basic factor in so many cases of angina pectoris" (Osler, 1910).

Returning to the idea of temporary distortion as the immediate consequence of stress, a later researcher, Cannon, draws attention to the object's "natural" (homeostatic or "systemic equilibration") tendency to resist. This he observed in his laboratory experiments on the "fight or flight" reaction. He described his subjects (humans and animals) as being "under stress" when they displayed certain reactions of the adrenal medulla and the sympathetic nervous system in the situations of cold, lack of oxygen, excitement, etc., to which he exposed them (Cannon, 1935). That the same endocrine reactions could be elicited by a wide variety of damaging or alarming stimuli prompted Hans Selye to postulate a "general adaptation syndrome" of somatic systems produced by "nonspecific stress." Selye (1946) postulated three stages in the G.A.S.:

> *Alarm reaction* in which an initial shock phase of lowered resistance is followed by countershock during which the individual's defense mechanisms become active
>
> *Resistance*—the stage of maximum adaptation and, hopefully, successful return to equilibrium for the individual. If, however, the stressor continues or defense does not work he will move on to
>
> *Exhaustion* when adaptive mechanisms collapse.

This framework (see Figure 1.2) brings out a distinction between short- and long-term implications of harm already touched on above and suggests that ultimate outcomes, even of stress, can be beneficial. In current usage

Figure 1.2

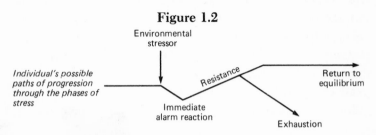

4

the immediate discomfort and anxiety are typically referred to as "the stress reaction," while long-term sufferings are viewed as consequences of stress.

Selye's work, while of considerable importance, was somewhat restricted to the stimulus-response laboratory setting. For a more relevant formulation to the theme of this book, we must turn to his contemporary, Wolff, who was concerned with describing stress as an inherent characteristic of life: "Since stress is a dynamic state within an organism in response to a demand for adaptation, and since life itself entails constant adaptation, living creatures are continually in a state of more or less stress" (Wolff, 1968). Having generalized the concept, Wolff is, however, alert to its individualistic nature; he placed considerable importance on the idea that different stressors will have different meanings for individuals in line with the latter's past experience. The modern theorist who has contributed most along these lines is Lazarus (1966, 1971). While pointing out that both the environmental stimulus and the reacting individual are vital elements (one cannot refer to a stimulus as such unless it is part of a reactive situation, etc.), he emphasizes that it is the nature of the relationship between the two which is crucial: "Stress refers, then, to a very broad class of problems differentiated from other problem areas because it deals with *any demands which tax the system,* whatever it is, a physiological system, a social system, or a psychological system, *and the response of that system*" (Lazarus, 1971). He goes on to say that the "reaction depends on how the person interprets or appraises (consciously or unconsciously) the significance of a harmful, threatening or challenging event."

"Cognitive appraisal" is an essentially individual-based affair: "The appraisal of threat is not a simple perception of the elements of the situation, but a judgment, an inference in which the data are assembled to a constellation of ideas and expectations" (Lazarus, 1966). Change in any one element—e.g., the background situation against which the stimulus is perceived—can radically alter the perceiver's interpretation.

Modern writers have, then, broken free from the early preoccupation with external force and acknowledge that stress is essentially individually defined and must be understood with reference to characteristics of *both* the focal individual and his environment, as it is the outcome of a particular combination of the two (Figure 1.3). (In the interests of semantic clarity we shall, from now on, refer to the external or internal causative forces involved as "pressures" or "stressors" and the resulting state of the organism as "stress.")

Figure 1.3

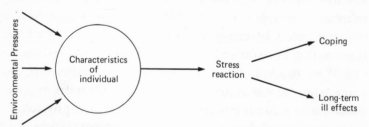

This general Person : Environment Fit paradigm will be taken up in later chapters and applied specifically to managerial job stress. Here it is important to note the two ways in which it differs radically from its engineering-based predecessor, which make it a more acceptable model of the real world. Firstly, by emphasizing the balance between P and E factors rather than absolute levels of either, it accommodates the finding that having too little to do can be as stressful for the organism as being overloaded. This is particularly important in the work context where career frustration and work underload have been identified as pressures. Secondly, it does not assume, as do alternative descriptions, that return to the preceding steady state is the only beneficial outcome possible. Stress can, therefore, be viewed as a stimulus to growth and the achievement of a new balance. Such a view has considerable commonsense appeal and receives support from researchers in other areas of the social sciences, for example, from sociologists dealing with "critical role transitions" (Parkes, 1971).

This shift of attention from the environment as a cause, to a particular Person: Environment combination as a trigger to stress, does, however, present problems to anyone concerned with the latter's identification. Measurement of a particular external pressure (number of degrees below freezing in a study concerned with reactions to the cold, for example) does not tell the *subjective* "load" on the individual concerned. It has, therefore, become necessary to assess stress by looking at its manifestations in the individual's psychological, physical or behavioral operations (reports of being cold, shivering or lighting a fire). The problems of such measurement are considered and discussed briefly in chapter 8. The remaining sections of this chapter deal with some of the ways that stress can be identified at this operational level.

7

THE HUMAN COSTS OF STRESS

His experiences and symptoms are an indication of the cost of stress to the individual. In the literature we find extensive discussion of criteria manifestations, particularly from those with a "company doctor" perspective. It is, however, to fiction that we must turn for the most convincing and well drawn profiles of individuals under stress. Here we shall draw briefly on the insights of three authors who describe managerial job stress.

Sloan Wilson (1972) wrote for a particular generation of American executives and much of his content—along with the uniform of its time, the gray flannel suit—is already dated. Many of his themes are, however, acquiring a new relevance as the norms of Western society develop —the gulf between the ambitious "workaholic" and his family is particularly important in the context of women's emancipation and has recently received considerable attention (Seidenberg, 1973; Packard, 1975). A more relevant work for today is *Something Happened* (1975) by Joseph Heller. Heller's powerful prose covers a wide range of possible job pressures experienced by his middle-aged executive hero and his colleagues. He does so carefully, however, in that he does not play down the compensatory, so often overriding, opportunities for satisfaction and achievement work provides. When describing his hero's work load, for example, Heller acknowledges in adjoining paragraphs both the frustration of underload

I am bored with my work very often now. Everything routine that comes in I pass along to somebody else.

This makes my boredom worse. It's a real problem to decide whether it's more boring to do something boring than to pass along everything boring that comes in to somebody else and then have nothing to do at all.

and the challenging stress of overload

Actually I enjoy my work when the assignments are large and urgent and somewhat frightening and will come to the attention of many people. I get scared, and am unable to sleep at night, but I usually perform at my best under this stimulating kind of pressure and enjoy my job the most. I handle all of these important projects myself, and I rejoice with tremendous pride and vanity in the compliments I receive when I do them well (as I always do). But between such peaks of challenge and elation there is monotony and despair.

Working in large organizations requires continual interaction with one's fellow employees; Heller, agreeing with Sartre that "hell is other people," describes the stress that relationships can cause:

In my department, there are six people who are afraid of me, and one small secretary who is afraid of all of us. I have one other person working for me who is not afraid of anyone, not even me, and I would fire him quickly, but I'm afraid of him.

He goes on to describe the interpersonal problems of one executive in more detail:

> Kagle is not comfortable with people on his own level or higher. He tends to sweat on his forehead and upper lip, and to bubble in the corners of his mouth. He feels he doesn't belong with them. He is not much at ease with people who work for him. He tries to pass himself off as one of them. This is a gross (and gauche) mistake, for his salesmen and branch managers don't want him to identify with them. To them, he is management; and they know that they are nearly wholly at his mercy. . . ."

Both academic and fiction writers depict managers as being more growth oriented than security oriented. Career progress becomes particularly problematic for the middle-aged manager who is running out of opportunities:

> Green is a clever tactician with long experience at office politics. He is a talented, articulate, intelligent man of fifty-six and has been with the company more than thirty years. He was a young man when he came here; he will soon be old. He has longed from the beginning to become a vice president and now knows that he will never succeed. He continues to yearn and he continues to strive and scheme, sometimes cunningly, other times desperately, objectly, ineptly, because he can neither admit nor deny to himself for very long that he has already failed.

Heller is as aware in his second novel as in his first of the way the individual is caught by the norms of the society in which he lives. Bob Slocum is punished by his job yet fears losing it; he sees no security in the policies of the organization for which he works:

> People in the company are almost never fired; if they grow inadequate or obsolete ahead of schedule, they are encouraged to retire early or are eased aside into hollow, insignificant, newly created positions with fake functions and no authority, where they are sheepish and unhappy for as long as they remain; nearly always, they must occupy a small and less convenient office, sometimes one with another person already in it; or, if they are still young, they are simply encouraged directly (although with courtesy) to find better jobs with other companies and then resign.

Other writers have suggested that such uncertainty is, in fact, inevitable in a society such as ours characterized by rapid change in things, places, people, information and organizations (Toffler, 1970; Taylor, 1972).

Many people are, however, so firmly tied into the system that they have no time to reflect deeply on what is happening to them. It is only at decision points that taken-for-granted pressures become salient. Middle age is just such a time of evaluation and reflection and appears to be a particularly critical time for the "average" manager (average in that he has not been strikingly more successful than the mass of his contemporaries). In his contribution to the literature, Nobbs (1976) captures the sense of frustration and disappointment of this age group to which so many academic writers allude:

> When I was young I looked with envy at grown-ups. People in their forties were solid, authoritative figures. . . . They were masters of the universe. . . . Well now I'm forty-six. But I don't feel solid and authoritative. I see the young strutting around like turkey cocks—self-assured, solid, terrifying. The question's this, isn't it? Do the young today see me as something solid and authoritative, were the people whom I thought so solid really feeling just like I am now? Or have I and my generation missed out? Have the tables been turned at exactly the wrong moment for us?

This brief selection has been drawn from a currently exploding pool of popular treatment of the effects of stress on managers. The recent proliferation of newspaper articles, TV plays, etc., on the topic suggest that it is a growing social problem. Hopefully, though, as taboos are lifted, as a society we may become better equipped to cope more successfully.

Manifestations of Stress

Taking a more academic view of these human costs, it is important to consider what stress means for the *functioning* of the individual concerned—that is, what symptoms does he display, and how can he and we, as friends and researchers, recognize his condition? Each individual will have his own distinctive repertoire of stress symptoms, just as he does his behaviors in any other type of situation. Manifestations of stress can be looked for at three levels of operation—the psychological, the physical and the behavioral.

Anxiety is one of the first and most important signs that an individual feels unable to cope. Even if he tries to hide this symptom, he will probably find concentrating and thinking clearly difficult and will tend to focus on short- rather than long-term outcomes. Being preoccupied with his problems, he may become irritable and find that he is unable to relax. Minor physical ailments— a headache, an upset stomach or a sleeping problem—are also among the early signs of trouble. If external pressure is persistent, the individual may develop more severe psychologically mediated symptoms—an ulcer, high blood pressure, shingles. Not only early symptoms but also attempts to cope either with the problem itself or its manifestations are signs of stress; behavioral symptoms are usually of this type. The manager may withdraw from those relationships which are proving difficult. He may smoke or drink more than usual in an attempt to relieve the tension. He may consult his doctor and find that he needs to take tranquilizers to help him through a particularly difficult time. Symptoms at each of these three levels can feed back to become causes of stress in their turn. Worries about his inabilities to concentrate or deteriorations in his health will be an added burden to the already stressed manager. Trying to solve problems in one life area (his work), he may cause further trouble by neglecting the demands of another (usually his home life).

The exact nature of the links between these initial signs and symptoms and the two ultimate criteria of stress —cardiovascular heart disease (CHD) and mental breakdown—is still openly and loudly debated. We shall, therefore, leave our treatment of symptomatology here. It is a broad and complex field which we have chosen to cover only superficially to give the reader an appreciation of what "being stressed" is taken to mean in the chapters which follow.

The Economic Costs of Stress

For our final perspective on the definition of stress, we turn from its cost in terms of human suffering to its cost to the national economy. This can be measured in only very broad terms but calculated by any available method can be seen to be considerable. United States studies estimate the incidence of mental illness in the population at approximately 10 percent (e.g., Gurin, Veroff and Feld, 1960). Translating this into accountable items such as loss of production, treatment, prevention and the damage done by illegal behavior, writers arrive at estimates (for the mid-1960s) of between six and twenty billion dollars per year (McMurray, 1973a and Conley et al., 1973, respectively) or 1 to 3 percent of the gross national product.

At a less spectacular level, other calculations suggest the following:

1. Stress costs substantially more than industrial injury.
2. Stress costs more than strikes (Gillespie, 1974).

Stress is, then, significant for both its human and economic costs. The rest of this book will go on to identify that substantial section of its causes which originate in the work environment as they interact with and affect the characteristics of one particular occupational group—managers—and look at how both individuals and companies might approach coping with them.

2
THE STRESSORS ON MANAGERS AT WORK: AN OVERVIEW

The success of any effort to minimize stress and maximize job satisfaction for managers will depend on accurate diagnosis, for different stressors will require different action. Any approach to stress reduction in an organization which relied on one particular approach (e.g., transcendental meditation or job enrichment) without taking into account the differences within work groups or divisions would be doomed to failure. A recognition of the possible sources of management stress, therefore, may help us to arrive at suggestions of ways of minimizing its negative consequences. It was with this in mind that we decided to bring together the research literature in the field of management and organizational stress in a framework that would help to more clearly identify sources of stress on managers.

One of the main problems currently facing research workers in the field of stress is that there is no integrated framework or conceptual map of the area. Much of the early stress research came from two sources. First, from work carried out in crisis situations such as stress in battle situations during wars, the stress effects of major illness or bereavement, etc., which focused heavily on the assessment of physical and mental symptoms exhibited in these unique circumstances. Second, from the occupational health literature which was geared essentially to the needs of industry and based to a large extent on intuition rather than substantiated fact. These studies were usually descriptive reports by individual industrial medical officers on, for example, the relationship of poor physical conditions at work and worker apathy or stress, or of work overload and nervous complaints by workers and managers, etc. In the last ten to fifteen years, however, there has been a determined effort by social scientists to consider more systematically the sources of management and organizational stress (Cooper and Marshall, 1976). The framework offered in this chapter is basically an attempt to integrate the findings of this new wave of research. Much of this work will be in the field of managerial stress. However, from an examination of the blue collar studies, it would appear that most of the factors to be discussed here are applicable to the labor force as a whole.

A study of the literature reveals a formidable list of over forty interacting factors which might be sources of managerial stress; those to be dealt with here were drawn mainly from a wider body of theory and research in a variety of fields: medicine, psychology, management sciences, etc.* Seven major categories of stress can be

*Some of the research literature reviewed here was drawn from an article published by the authors in the *Journal of Occupational Psychology* 49, 1976, pp. 11–28.

identified, six external and one internal to the manager concerned. Figure 2.1 is an attempt to represent these diagrammatically; below they will be dealt with in turn. The external categories will be discussed first in a natural progression from immediate job- to total environment-related; the individual's personal contribution will then be considered.

FACTORS INTRINSIC TO THE JOB

Factors intrinsic to the job were a first and vital focus of study for early researchers in the field, and in blue collar (as opposed to management) studies are still the main preoccupation. Stress can be caused by too much or too little work, time pressures and deadlines, having too many decisions (Sofer, 1970), fatigue from the physical strains of the work environment (e.g., assembly line), excessive travel, long hours, having to cope with changes at work and the expenses (monetary and career) of making mistakes (Kearns, 1973). It can be seen that every job description includes factors which for some individuals at some point will be a source of pressure. Two factors have received the major part of research effort in this area (the others being more speculative than proven sources of stress): working conditions and work overload.

Working Conditions

A great deal of work has been done linking the working conditions of a particular job to physical and mental

18

Figure 2.1 Sources of managerial stress

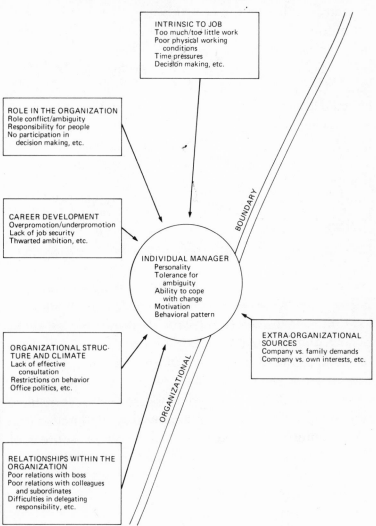

health. Kornhauser (1965) found, for example, that poor mental health was directly related to unpleasant work conditions, the necessity to work fast and to expend a lot of physical effort, and to excessive and inconvenient hours. There is increasing evidence (Marcson, 1970; Shepard, 1971) that physical health, as well, is adversely affected by repetitive and dehumanizing environments (e.g., paced assembly lines). Kritsikis, Heinemann and Eitner (1968) in a study of 150 men with angina pectoris in a population of over 4,000 industrial workers in Berlin reported that a larger number of these workers came from work environments employing conveyor-line systems than any other work technology.

Work Overload

A more important stressor for managers than working conditions is work overload. Research into work overload has been given substantial empirical attention. French and Caplan (1973) have differentiated overload in terms of *quantitative* and *qualitative* overload. Quantitative refers to having too much to do, while qualitative means work that is too difficult. (The complementary phenomena of quantitative and qualitative underload are also hypothesized as potential sources of stress but with little or no supportive research evidence.) Miller (1960) has theorized that overload in most systems leads to breakdown, whether we are dealing with single biological cells or managers in organizations. In an early study, French and Caplan (1970) found that objective quantitative overload was strongly linked to cigarette smoking (an important risk factor or symptom of coronary heart disease). Persons with more phone calls, office visits, and meetings per given unit of work time were found to smoke significantly more cigarettes than persons with fewer such engagements. In a study of 100 young coronary patients, Russek and Zohman (1958) found that 25 percent had been working at two jobs and an additional 45 percent had worked at jobs which required (due to work overload) 60 or more hours per week. They add that although prolonged emotional strain preceded the attack in 91 percent of the cases, similar stress was only observed in 20 percent of the controls. Buell and Breslow (1960) have also reported findings which support a relationship between hours of work and death from coronary disease. In an investigation of mortality rates of men in California, they observed that workers in light industry under the age of 45, who are on the job more than 48 hours a week, have twice the risk of death from CHD compared with similar workers working 40 or less hours a week. Another substantial investigation on quantitative work load was carried out by Margolis, Kroes and Quinn (1974) on a representative national sample of 1,496 employed persons, 16 years of age or older. They found that overload was significantly related to a number of symptoms or indicators of stress: escapist drinking, absenteeism from work, low motivation to work, lowered self-esteem, and an absence of suggestions to employers. The results from these and other studies (Quinn, Seashore, and Mangione, 1971; Porter and Lawler, 1965) are relatively consistent and indicate that this factor is indeed a potential source of occupational stress that adversely affects both health and job satisfaction.

There is also some evidence that (for some occupations) qualitative overload is a source of stress, and this is particularly relevant to managers. French, Tupper and Mueller (1965) looked at qualitative and quantitative work overload in a large university. They used questionnaires, interviews and medical examinations to obtain data on risk factors associated with coronary heart disease for 122 university administrators and professors. They found that one symptom of stress, low self-esteem, was related to work overload but that this was different for the two occupational groupings. Qualitative overload was not significantly linked to low self-esteem among the administrators but was significantly correlated for the professors. The greater the quality of work expected of the professor the lower the self-esteem. They also found that qualitative and quantitative overload were correlated to achievement orientation. And, more interestingly, in a follow-up study that achievement orientation correlated very strongly with serum uric acid (Brooks and Mueller, 1966). Several other studies have reported an association of qualitative work overload with cholesterol level: a tax deadline for accountants (Friedman, Rosenman and Carroll, 1958), and medical students performing a medical examination under observation (Dreyfuss and Czaczkes, 1959). French and Caplan (1973) summarize this research by suggesting that both qualitative and quantitative overload produce at least nine different symptoms of psychological and physical strain: job dissatisfaction, job tension, lower self-esteem, threat, embarrassment, high cholesterol levels, increased heart rate, skin resistance, and more smoking. In analyzing this data, however, one cannot ignore the vital interactive relationship of the job and manager or employee; objective work overload, for example, should not be viewed in isolation but relative to the individual's capacities and personality.

Such caution is sanctioned by much of the literature which shows that overload is not always externally imposed. Many managers (perhaps certain personality types more than others) react to overload by working longer hours. Uris (1972), for example, reports on a study in which it was found that 45 percent of the executives investigated worked all day, in the evenings, and on weekends, and that a further 37 percent kept weekends free but worked extra hours in the evenings. In many companies this type of behavior has become a norm to which everyone feels they must adhere.

ROLE IN THE ORGANIZATION

Another major source of managerial stress is a person's role at work. A great deal of research in this area has concentrated on role ambiguity and role conflict, since the seminal investigations of the Survey Research Center of the University of Michigan which were reported in the classic book *Organizational Stress: Studies in Role Conflict and Ambiguity* (Kahn, Wolfe, Quinn, Snoek and Rosenthal, 1964).

23

Role Ambiguity

Role ambiguity exists when an individual has inadequate information about his work role, that is, where there is *lack of clarity* about the work objectives associated with the role, about colleagues' expectation of the work role and about the scope and responsibilities of the job. Kahn et al. found in their study that men who suffered from role ambiguity experienced lower job satisfaction, higher job-related tension, greater futility, and lower self-confidence. French and Caplan (1970) found, at one of NASA's bases (Goddard Space Flight Center), in a sample of 205 volunteer engineers, scientists and administrators that role ambiguity was significantly related to low job satisfaction and to feelings of job-related threat to one's mental and physical well-being. This also related to indicators of physiological strain such as increased blood pressure and pulse rate. Margolis, Kroes and Quinn (1974) also found a number of significant relationships between symptoms or indicators of physical and mental ill health with role ambiguity in their representative national sample (n = 1496). The stress indicators related to role ambiguity were depressed mood, lowered self-esteem, life dissatisfaction, job dissatisfaction, low motivation to work, and intention to leave the job. These were not very strong relationships but, nevertheless, statistically significant, and they do indicate that lack of role clarity may be one among many potential stressors at work.

Kahn (1973) feels that it is now time to separate out distinctive elements of role ambiguity for individual treatment (just as he and his research team have done for overload and responsibility). He suggests that two components are involved—those of present ambiguity and future prospects of ambiguity (much of the material he assigns to the latter is here classified as career development stress)—but he has not yet empirically substantiated this differentiation.

Role Conflict

Role conflict exists when an individual in a particular work role is torn by conflicting job demands or by having to do things he/she really does not want to do or does not think are part of the job specification. The most frequent manifestation of this is when a person is caught between two groups of people who demand different kinds of behavior or expect that the job should entail different functions. Kahn et al. found that men who suffered more role conflict had lower job satisfaction and higher job-related tension. It is interesting to note that they also found that the greater the power or authority of the people "sending" the conflicting role messages, the more role conflict produced job dissatisfaction. This was related to physiological strain as well, as the Goddard study (French and Caplan, 1970) illustrates. They telemetered and recorded the heart rate of twenty-two men for a two-hour period while they were at work in their offices. They found that the mean heart rate for an individual was strongly related to his report of role conflict.

A larger and medically more sophisticated study by Shirom, Eden, Silberwasser and Kellermann (1973) found similar results. Their research is of particular interest because it tried to look simultaneously at a wide variety of potential stressors. They collected data on 762 male kibbutz members aged 30 and above, drawn from 13 kibbutzim throughout Israel. They examined the relationships between CHD (myocardial infarction, angina pectoris, and coronary insufficiency), abnormal electrocardiographic readings, CHD risk factors (systolic blood pressure, pulse rate, serum cholesterol levels, etc.) and potential sources of occupational stress (work overload, role ambiguity, role conflict, lack of physical activity). Their data was broken down by occupational groups: agricultural workers, factory groups, craftsmen, and white collar workers. It was found that there was a significant relationship between role conflict and CHD (specifically, abnormal electrocardiographic readings) but for the white collar workers only. In fact, as we move down the ladder from occupations requiring great physical exertion (e.g., agriculture) to least (e.g., white collar), the greater was the relationship between role ambiguity/conflict and abnormal electrocardiographic findings. Role conflict was also significantly related to an index of ponderosity (excessive weight for age and height). It was also found that in going from occupations involving excessive physical activities to those with less such activity, CHD (myocardial infarction, angina pectoris, and coronary insufficiency) increased significantly. Drawing together this data, it might be hypothesized that people in managerial and professional occupations are more likely to suffer occupational stress from role-related stress and other interpersonal dynamics and less from the physical conditions of work.

A more quantified measure of role conflict itself is

found in research reported by Mettlin and Woelfel (1974). They measured three aspects of interpersonal influence—discrepancy between influences, level of influence and number of influences—in a study of the educational and occupational aspirations of high school students. Using the Langner Stress Symptom questionnaire as their index of stress, they found that the more extensive and diverse an individual's interpersonal communications network the more stress symptoms he showed. The organizational role which is at a boundary—i.e., between departments or between the company and the outside world—is, by definition, one of extensive communication nets and of high role conflict. Kahn et al. suggested that such a position is potentially highly stressful. Other researchers have provided empirical support for this suggestion; Margolis and Kroes (1974), for example, found that foremen (high role-conflict prone job) are seven times as likely to develop ulcers as blue collar workers.

Responsibility

Another important potential stressor associated with one's organizational role is responsibility. One can differentiate here between responsibility for people and responsibility for things (equipment, budgets, etc.). Wardwell, Hyman and Bahnson (1964) found that responsibility for people was significantly more likely to lead to CHD than responsibility for things. Increased responsibility for people frequently means that one has to spend more time interacting with others, attending meetings, working alone and, in consequence, as in the Goddard study, more

27

time in trying to meet deadline pressures and schedules. Pincherle (1972) also found this in his study of 2,000 executives attending a center for a medical check-up. Of the 1,200 managers sent by their companies for their annual examination, there was evidence of physical stress being linked to age and level of responsibility; the older and more responsible the executive, the greater the probability of the presence of CHD risk factors or symptoms. Other research (Terhure, 1963) has also established this link. The relationship between age and stress-related illness could be explained, however, by the fact that as the executive gets older he may be troubled by stressors other than increased responsibility, for example, as Eaton (1969) suggests, by (1) a recognition that further advancement is unlikely, (2) increasing isolation and narrowing of interests and (3) an awareness of approaching retirement. Nevertheless, the finding by French and Caplan in the Goddard study does indicate that responsibility for people must play some part in the process of stress, particularly for clerical, managerial and professional workers. They found that responsibility for people was significantly related to heavy smoking, diastolic blood pressure, and serum cholesterol levels—the more the individual had responsibility for things as opposed to people the lower were each of these CHD risk factors.

Other Role Stressors

Having too little responsibility (Brook, 1973), lack of participation in decision making, lack of managerial support, having to keep up with increasing standards of performance and coping with rapid technological change are other potential role stressors mentioned repeatedly in the literature but with little supportive research evidence. Variations between organizational structures will determine the differential distribution of these factors across differing occupational groups. Kay (1974) does suggest, however, that (independent of the employing organization) some pressures are to be found more at middle-management levels than at other levels. He depicts today's middle manager as being particularly hard pressed by

1. Pay compression, as the salaries of new recruits increase
2. Job insecurity—they are particularly vulnerable to redundancy or forced, premature retirement
3. Having little real authority at their high levels of responsibility
4. Feeling "boxed in"

When interviewed, it is those pressures intrinsic to the job and due to their role in the organization which managers consider to be the most legitimate sources of stress vis-a-vis their jobs. Typically, they are referred to as "what I'm paid for," "why I'm here," and even when they cause severe disruption, the implication is that they cannot be legitimately avoided. In many companies, in fact, there are institutional ways in which these problems can be handled; for example, deadlines are set unrealistically early to allow a margin of error, decisions are made by groups so that no one individual has to take full responsibility, the employee is allowed to neglect certain tasks (e.g., filing) if he is busy, work can be reallocated within a department if one member is seen to be doing more than his fair share. The manager, however, may not always perceive himself as free to use these fail-safe mechanisms.

RELATIONSHIPS WITHIN THE ORGANIZATION

A third major source of stress at work has to do with the nature of relationships with one's boss, subordinates and colleagues. A number of behavioral scientists (Argyris, 1964; Cooper, 1973) have suggested that good relationships between members of a work group are a central factor in individual and organizational health. Nevertheless, very little research work has been done in this area to either support or disprove this hypothesis. French and Caplan (1973) define poor relations as "those which include low trust, low supportiveness, and low interest in listening to and trying to deal with problems that confront the organizational member." The most notable studies in this area are by Kahn et al. (1964), French and Caplan (1970), and Buck (1972). Both the Kahn et al. and French and Caplan studies came to roughly the same conclusion: that mistrust of persons one worked with was positively related to high role ambiguity, which led to inadequate communications between people and to "psychological strain in the form of low job satisfaction and to feelings of job-related threat to one's well-being." It was interesting

30

to note, however, in the Kahn study that poor relations with one's subordinates was significantly related to feelings of threat with colleagues and superiors but not in regard to threat with subordinates.

Relationships with Superior

Buck (1972) focused on the attitude and relationship of workers and managers to their immediate boss using Fleishman's leadership questionnaire on consideration and initiating structure. The consideration factor was associated with behavior indicative of friendship, mutual trust, respect and a certain warmth between boss and subordinate. He found that those workers who felt that their boss was low on consideration reported feeling more job pressure. Workers who were under pressure reported that their bosses did not give them criticism in a helpful way, played favorites with subordinates, "pulled rank and took advantage of them whenever they got a chance." Buck concludes that the "considerate behavior of supervisors appears to have contributed significantly (inversely) to feelings of job pressure."

Relationships with Subordinates

Officially, one of the most critical functions of a manager is his supervision of other people's work. It has long been accepted that an inability to delegate might be a problem, but now a new potential stressor is being introduced in the manager's interpersonal skills—he must learn to manage by participation. Donaldson and Gowler (1975) point to the factors which may make today's zealous emphasis on participation a cause of resentment, anxiety and stress for the manager:

1. Mismatch of formal and actual power
2. Resentment of the erosion of his formal role and authority (and the loss of status and rewards)
3. Being subject to irreconcilable pressures, e.g., to be both participative and to achieve high production
4. Refusal of subordinates to participate

Particularly for those with technical and scientific backgrounds (a "things orientation"), relationships can be a low priority (seen as trivial, time consuming and an impediment to doing the job well) and one would expect their interactions to be more a source of stress than those of people-oriented managers.

Relationships with Colleagues

Besides the obvious factors of office politics and colleague rivalry, we find another element here: stress can be caused not only by the pressure of relationships but also by its opposite—a lack of adequate social support in difficult situations (Lazarus, 1966). At highly competitive managerial levels it is likely that problem sharing will be inhibited for fear of appearing weak; much of the literature particularly mentions the isolated life of the top executive as an added source of strain.

Morris (1975) encompasses this whole area of rela-

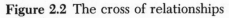
Figure 2.2 The cross of relationships

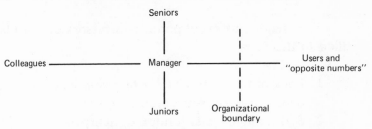

tionships in one model—what he calls the "cross of relationships" (Figure 2.2). While he acknowledges the differences between relationships on the various continua, he feels that the focal manager must bring all four into dynamic balance in order to be able to deal with the stress of his position. Morris' suggestion seems only sensible when we realize that the manager spends a high proportion of his work time with other people. In a research program to find out exactly what managers do, Minzberg (1973) showed just how much time is spent in interaction. In an intensive study of a small sample of chief executives, he found that in a large organization a mere 22 percent of time was spent in desk work, the rest being taken up by telephone calls (6 percent), scheduled meetings (59 percent), unscheduled meetings (10 percent) and other activities (3 percent). In small organizations basic desk work played a larger part (52 percent), but nearly 40 percent was still devoted to face-to-face contacts of one kind or another. Despite its obvious importance and the inclusion of relationship measures in many multivariate studies, there is little in-depth research available in this area.

33

CAREER DEVELOPMENT

Two major clusters of potential stressors can be identified in this area:

1. Lack of job security (fear of redundancy, obsolescence or early retirement, etc.)
2. Status incongruity (under- or overpromotion, frustration at having reached one's career ceiling, etc.)

For many managers their career progression is of overriding importance—by promotion they earn not only more money but also a higher status and the new job challenges for which they strive. Typically, in the early years at work, this striving and the aptitude to come to terms quickly with a rapidly changing environment is fostered and suitably rewarded by the company. Career progression is, perhaps, a problem by its very nature; for example, Sofer (1970) found that many of his sample believed that luck and being in the right place at the right time play a major role.

At middle age, and usually middle-management levels, a career becomes more problematic and most executives find their progress slowed, if not actually stopped. Job opportunities become fewer, those jobs that are available take longer to master, past (mistaken?) decisions cannot be revoked, old knowledge and methods become obsolete, energies may be flagging or demanded for family activities and there is the press of fresh young recruits to face in competition. Both Levinson (1973) and Constandse (1972)—the latter refers to this phase as "the male

34

menopause"—depict the manager as suffering these fears and disappointments in silent isolation from his family and work colleagues.

The fear of demotion or obsolescence can be strong for those who know they have reached their career ceiling, and most will inevitably suffer some erosion of status before they finally retire. Goffman (1952), extrapolating from a technique employed in the con game ("cooling the mark out"), suggests that the company should bear some of the responsibility for taking the sting out of this (felt) failure experience.

From the company perspective, on the other hand, McMurray (1973b) establishes a case for not promoting a manager to a higher position if there is doubt that he can fill it. In a syndrome he labels the "executive neurosis," he describes the overpromoted manager as grossly overworking to keep down a top job while at the same time hiding his insecurity. McMurray points to the consequences of this for the manager's work performance and the company. Age is no longer revered as it was—management is increasingly becoming a young man's world. The rapidity with which society is developing (technologically, economically and socially) is likely to mean that individuals will now need to change careers during their working life (as companies and products are having to do). Such trends breed uncertainty, and research suggests that older workers look for stability (Sleeper, 1975). Unless managers adapt their expectations to suit new circumstances, career-development stress, especially in later life, is likely to become an increasingly common experience.

Erikson and Gunderson of the U.S. Navy Neuropsychiatric Unit are developing a comprehensive research program in the U.S. navy to assess one facet of career-development stress which they term "status congruence" or the more systematic matching of one individual's advancement with his experience and ability. In an earlier study they (Arthur and Gunderson, 1965) found that promotional lag was significantly related to psychiatric illness. Later they (Erikson, Pugh and Gunderson, 1972) found that navy personnel experienced greater job satisfaction when their rates of advancement exceeded (although not excessively) their expectation; dissatisfaction increased as advancement rates were retarded. Those who were least successful with regard to advancement tended to perceive the greatest amount of stress in their lives. In a more recent study Erikson, Edwards and Gunderson (1973) found among a sample of over 9,000 navy ratings that status congruency was (1) negatively related to the incidence of psychiatric disorder and (2) positively related to military effectiveness.

The issue of status congruency has also been researched from a sociological perspective, that is, the incongruity between an individual's social status and that of his parents, or social class differences between his parents. Shekelle, Ostfeld and Paul (1969), for example, in a prospective study of a medically examined industrial population, discovered that men were at a significantly higher risk of CHD when their social class in childhood, or the wife's social class in her childhood, was higher or lower than the class level that they presently shared. Kasl and Cobb (1967) also found that parental status stress appears to be a variable having "strong, long-term effects on physical and mental health of adult offspring." Berry (1966) found among a 6,131 national sample that a small amount of variance in morbidity rate (incidence of hospitalization) was explained by status inconsistency. Jackson (1962) reached a more differentiated conclusion about status incongruence "that all forms of status inconsistency are psychologically disturbing, but response to stress varies with relative positions of the inconsistent person's achieved and ascribed status ranks." More and more evidence is growing that social status stress is a problem in Western, highly mobile society. As Wan (1971) summarizes, the rationale for stress induced by status inconsistency is that "role conflict generated from incompatible expectations of a social position may yield psychological disturbances and frustrations which in turn form part of the stress-disease linkage."

ORGANIZATIONAL STRUCTURE AND CLIMATE

A fifth potential source of managerial stress is simply being in the organization and the threat to an individual's freedom, autonomy and identity this poses. Problem areas such as little or no participation in the decision-making process, no sense of belonging, lack of effective consultation, poor communications, restrictions on behavior, and office politics are some of the more impactful ones here. An increasing number of research investigations are being conducted in this area, particularly into the effect of employee participation in the workplace. This research

37

development is contemporaneous to a growing movement in North America and in the EEC countries of worker participation programs involving autonomous work groups, worker directors, and a greater sharing of the decision-making process throughout the organization. The early work on participation was in terms of its effect on production and attitudes of workers. For example, Coch and French (1948) examined the degrees of participation in a sewing factory. They found the greater the participation the higher was the productivity, the greater the job satisfaction, the lower the turnover and the better were the relationships between boss and subordinate. These findings were later supported by a field experiment in a footwear factory in southern Norway where greater participation led to significantly more favorable attitudes by workers toward management and more involvement in their jobs (French, Israel and As, 1960).

The research more relevant to our interests here, however, is the recent work on lack of participation and stress-related disease. In the Goddard study French and Caplan (1970), for example, found that people who reported greater opportunities for participation in decision making also reported significantly greater job satisfaction, lower job-related feelings of threat and higher feelings of self-esteem. Buck (1972) found that both managers and workers who felt under pressure the most reported that their supervisors "always ruled with an iron hand and rarely tried out new ideas or allowed participation in decision making." Managers who were under stress also reported that their supervisors never let the persons under them do their work in the way they thought best. Among a national representative sample of over 1,400 workers, Margolis, Kroes and Quinn (1974) found that nonparticipation at work was the most consistent and significant predictor or indicator of strain and job-related stress. They found that nonparticipation was significantly related to the following health risk factors: overall poor physical health, escapist drinking, depressed mood, low self-esteem, low life satisfaction, low job satisfaction, low motivation to work, intention to leave job, and absenteeism from work. Kasl (1973) also found that low job satisfaction was related to nonparticipation in decision making, inability to provide feedback to supervisors and lack of recognition for good performance; and that poor mental health was linked to close supervision and no autonomy at work (Quinn, Seashore and Mangione, 1971). Neff (1968) has highlighted the importance of lack of participation and involvement by suggesting that "mental health at work is to a large extent a function of the degree to which output is under the control of the individual workers." To summarize, the research above seems to indicate that greater participation leads to lower staff turnover, higher productivity, and that when participation is absent, lower job satisfaction and higher levels of physical and mental health risks may result.

We have seen (Donaldson and Gowler, 1975), however, that it may be difficult to satisfy the needs of all levels of the work force with the *same* change program. There is, therefore, reason to approach this topic with caution, particularly as the studies quoted relied on correlational analysis for their conclusions and the inferences to causality that can be drawn are limited.

39

EXTRA-ORGANIZATIONAL SOURCES OF STRESS

The sixth and final source of external job stress is more of a catchall for all those interfaces between life outside and life inside the organization that might put pressure on the manager; family problems (Pahl and Pahl, 1971), life crises (Dohrenwend and Dohrenwend, 1974), financial difficulties, conflict of personal beliefs with those of the company and the conflict of company with family demands. Despite repeated calls to researchers to acknowledge that the individual "functions as a totality" (Wright, 1975a), the practical problems of encompassing the whole person in one research plan usually leave those who try with either incomprehensibly complex results or platitudinous generalizations. Most studies, then, have only one life area as the focus of study.

The extra-organizational area which has received most research interest is that of the manager's relationship with his wife and family. (It is widely agreed that managers have little time for outside activities apart from their families. Writers who have examined their effects on the local community (Packard, 1972) have pointed to the disruptive consequences of the executive's lack of involvement.) The manager has two main problems vis-a-vis his family:

1. Management of his time and commitments. Not only does his busy life leave him few resources with which to cope with other people's needs, but in order to do his job well the manager usually also needs support from others to cope with the back-

ground chores of housekeeping and maintenance, to relieve stress when possible and to maintain contact with the outside world.

2. Often a result of the first is the spillover of crises or stresses in one system which affect the other.

As these two are inseparable, we shall go on to discuss them together.

Marriage Patterns

The arrangement the manager comes to with his wife will be of vital importance to both problem areas. Pahl and Pahl (1971) found that the majority of wives in their middle-class sample saw their role in relation to their husbands' job as a supportive, domestic one; all said that they derived their sense of security from their husbands (only two men said the same of their wives). Barber (1976), in interviewing five directors' wives, found similar attitudes. Gowler and Legge (1975) have dubbed this bond "the hidden contract," in which the wife agrees to act as a support team so that her husband can fill the demanding job to which he aspires. Handy (1976) supports the idea that this is typical and that it is the path to career success for the manager concerned. Based on individual psychometric data, he describes a number of possible marriage-role combinations. In his sample of top executives (in mid-career) and their wives, he found that the most frequent pattern (about half the 22 couples interviewed) was the "thrusting male–caring female." This he depicts as highly role segregated with the emphasis on

41

separation, silence and complementary activities. Historically, both the company and the manager have reaped benefits from maintaining the segregation of work and home implicit in this pattern. The company thus legitimates its demand for a constant work performance from its employee, no matter what his home situation, and the manager is free to pursue his career but keeps a safe haven to which he can return to relax and recuperate. The second and most frequent combination was "involved–involved"—a dual-career pattern with the emphasis on complete sharing. This, while potentially extremely fulfilling for both parties, requires energy inputs which might well prove so excessive that none of the roles involved are fulfilled successfully.

It is unlikely that the patterns described above will be negotiated explicitly or that they will in the long term be in balance. Major factors in their continuing evolution will be the work and family demands of particular life stages. A recent report (*The Management Threshold* by Beattie, Darlington and Cripps, 1974), for example, highlights the difficult situation of the young executive who, in order to build up his career, must devote a great deal of time and energy to his job just when his young housebound wife, with small children, is also making pressing demands. The report suggests that the executive fights to maintain the distance between his wife and the organization, so that she will not be in a position to evaluate the choices he has to make; paradoxically, he does so at a time when he is most in need of sympathy and understanding. Guest and Williams (1973) examined the complete career cycle in similar terms pointing out how the demands of the different systems change over time. The addition of role-disposition and personality-disposition variations to their equations would, however, make them even more valuable.

Mobility

Home conflicts become particularly critical in relation to managerial relocation and mobility. Much of the literature on this topic comes from the United States where mobility is a significant part of the national character.

At an individual level the effects of mobility on the manager's wife and family have been studied. Researchers agree that whether she is willing to move or not, the wife bears the brunt of relocations and conclude that most husbands do not appreciate what this involves. Writers point to signs that wives are suffering and becoming less cooperative. Immundo (1974) hypothesizes that increasing divorce rates can be seen as the upwardly aspiring manager races ahead of his socially unskilled stay-at-home wife. Seidenberg (1973) comments on the rise in the ratio of female to male alcoholics in the United States from $1:5$ in 1962 to $1:2$ in 1973 and asks the question "Do corporate wives have souls?" Descriptive accounts of the frustrations and loneliness of being a corporate wife proliferate. Increasing teenage delinquency and violence is also laid at the door of the mobile manager and the society which he has created.

Constant moving can have profound effects on the life-style of the people concerned, particularly on their relationships with others. Staying only two years or so in one place, mobile families do not have time to develop close ties with the local community. Immundo (1974) talks of the "mobility syndrome," a way of behaving geared to developing only temporary relationships. Packard (1975) describes ways in which individuals react to the type of fragmenting society this creates, e.g., treating everything as if it is temporary, being indifferent to local community amenities and organizations, living for the present and becoming adept at "instant gregariousness." He goes on to point out the likely consequences for local communities, the nation and the rootless people involved.

Pahl and Pahl (1971) suggest that many mobiles retreat into their nuclear family. This conclusion is supported, at a theoretical level, by Parsons (1943) who is concerned that this places even greater demands for stability, identity and emotional support on this, already often precarious, institution. Managers, particularly, do not become involved in local affairs due both to lack of time and to an appreciation that they are only short-stay inhabitants. Their wives find participation easier (especially in a mobile rather than a static area), and a recent survey suggested that for some, involvement is a necessity to compensate for their husbands' ambitions and career involvement which keep him away from home. From the company's point of view, the way in which a wife does adjust to her new environment can affect her husband's work performance. Guest and Williams (1973) illustrate this by an example of a major international company who, on surveying 1,800 of their executives in 70 countries, concluded that the two most important influences on overall satisfaction with the overseas assignment were the

44

job itself and, more importantly, the executives' wives adjustment to the foreign environment. Clinical evidence suggests that one partner's problems may even contribute to the mental ill health of the other.

Despite the importance of the work : home interface and the real problem that it poses to most managers and their wives at some time or another, there is a distinct lack of controlled research work to suggest how conflict affects both work performance and marriage or how crises or triumphs in one system feed back to influence the other.

CHARACTERISTICS OF THE INDIVIDUAL

Sources of pressure at work evoke different reactions from different people. Some people are better able to cope with these stressors than others; they adapt their behavior in a way that meets the environmental challenge. On the other hand, some people are more characterologically predisposed to stress, that is, they are unable to cope or adapt to the stress-provoking situation. Many factors may contribute to these differences—personality, motivation, being unable or ill equipped to deal with problems in a particular area of expertise, fluctuations in abilities (particularly with age), insight into one's own motivations and weaknesses, etc. It would be useful to examine, therefore, those characteristics of the individual that research evidence indicates are predisposers to stress. Most of the research in this area has focused on personality differences between high- and low-stressed individuals and has taken two principal directions: one has concentrated on examining the relationship between various psychometric measures primarily using the MMPI (Minnesota Multiphasic Personality Inventory) and 16 PF (Cattell's 16 Personality Factors scale) and stress-related disease (primarily coronary heart disease); and the other on stress- or coronary-prone behavior patterns and the incidence of disease. Jenkins (1971a, 1971b) provides an extensive and excellent review of these studies which we will summarize here.

Psychometric Measures

In the first category, there were six studies which utilized the MMPI. The result of these six studies (Bakker and Levenson, 1967; Ostfeld, Lebovits and Shekelle, 1964; Lebovits, Shekelle and Ostfeld, 1967; Brozek, Kays and Blackburn, 1966; Bruhn, Chandler and Wolf, 1969; Mordkoff and Rand, 1968) seems to be that before their illness patients with coronary disease differ from persons who remain healthy on several MMPI scales, particularly those in the neurotic triad of hypochondriasis (Hs), depression (D), and hysteria (Hy). The occurrence of manifest CHD increases the deviation of patients' MMPI scores further and, in addition, there is ego defense breakdown. As Jenkins (1971a) summarizes, "patients with fatal disease tend to show greater neuroticism (particularly depression) in prospective MMPIs than those who incur and survive coronary disease." There are three major studies utilizing the 16PF (Bakker, 1967; Finn, Hickey and O'Doherty, 1969; Lebovits, Shekelle and Ostfeld, 1967). All three of these report emotional instability (low Scale C), particularly for patients with angina pectoris. Two studies report high conformity and submissiveness (Factor E) and desurgency/seriousness (Factor F), and two report high self-sufficiency (Factor Q2). Bakker's angina patients are similar to Finn's sample with CHD in manifesting shyness (Factor H) and apprehensiveness (Factor O). The results from all three studies portray the patients with CHD or related illness as emotionally unstable and introverted, which is consistent with the six MMPI studies. The limitation of these studies is that they are, on balance, retrospective. That is, that anxiety and neuroticism may well be reactions to CHD and other stress-related illnesses rather than precursors of it. Paffenbarger, Wolf, and Notkin (1966) did an interesting prospective study in which they linked university psychometric data on students with death certificates filed years later. They found a number of significant precursors to fatal CHD, one of which was a high anxiety/neuroticism score for the fatal cases.

Kahn et al. (1964), adopting a more selective approach to personality measurement, came up with some more practically oriented results than those of the above general explorations. They examined a sample of managers on a series of personality variables—extroversion versus introversion, flexibility versus rigidity, inner versus outer directedness, open versus closed mindedness, achievement versus status versus security oriented—and related these to job stress. The following gives an indication of some of their results: (1) outer-directed people were more adaptable and more highly reality-oriented than inner-directed; (2) "rigids" and "flexibles" perceived

47

different types of situations as stressful, the former being more susceptible to rush jobs from above and dependence on other people, while the latter were more open to influence from other people, and thus easily became overloaded; (3) achievement-seekers showed significantly more independence and job involvement than did security-seekers.

Behavior Patterns

The other research approach to individual stress differences began with the work of Friedman and Rosenman (Friedman, 1969; Rosenman, Friedman and Strauss, 1964, 1966) and developed later showing a relationship between behavioral patterns and the prevalence of CHD. They found that individuals manifesting certain behavioral traits were significantly more at risk to CHD. These individuals were later referred to as the "coronary-prone behavior pattern Type A" as distinct from Type B (low risk of CHD). Type A was found to be the overt behavioral syndrome or style of living characterized by "extremes of competitiveness, striving for achievement, aggressiveness, haste, impatience, restlessness, hyperalertness, explosiveness of speech, tenseness of facial musculature and feelings of being under pressure of time and under the challenge of responsibility." It was suggested that "people having this particular behavioral pattern were often so deeply involved and committed to their work that other aspects of their lives were relatively neglected" (Jenkins, 1971b). In the early studies, persons were designated as Type A or Type B on the basis of clinical judgments of

48

doctors and psychologists or peer ratings. These studies found a higher incidence of CHD among Type A than Type B. Many of the inherent methodological weaknesses of this approach were overcome by the classic Western Collaborative Group Study (Rosenman, Friedman, and Strauss, 1964, 1966). It was prospective (as opposed to the earlier retrospective studies) and based on a national sample of over 3,400 men free of CHD. All these men were rated Type A or B by psychiatrists after intensive interviews, without knowledge of any biological data about them and without the individuals being seen by a heart specialist. Diagnosis was made by an electrocardiographer and an independent medical practitioner, who were not informed about the subjects' behavioral patterns. They found the following results: two and a half years after the start of the study, Type A men between the ages of 39–49 and 50–59, had 6.5 and 1.9 times, respectively, the incidence of CHD than Type B men. They also had the following risk factors of high serum cholesterol levels, elevated beta-lipoproteins, decreased blood clotting time, and elevated daytime excretion of norepinephrine. After four and a half years of the follow-up observation in the study, the *same* relationship of behavioral pattern and incidence of CHD was found. In terms of the clinical manifestations of CHD, individuals exhibiting Type A behavioral patterns had a significantly higher incidence of acute myocardial infarction (and of clinically unrecognized myocardial infarction) and angina pectoris. Rosenman, Friedman and Jenkins (1967) also found that the risk of recurrent and fatal myocardial infarction was significantly related to Type A characteristics. Quinlan and his

49

colleagues (Quinlan, Barrow and Hayes, 1969) found the same results among Trappist and Benedictine monks. Monks judged to be Type A coronary-prone cases (by a double-blind procedure) had 2.3 times the prevalence of angina and 4.3 times the prevalence of infarction as compared to monks judged Type B. Many other studies (Bortner and Rosenman, 1967; Zyzanski and Jenkins, 1970) have been conducted with roughly the same findings.

Researchers at the Institute of Social Research, University of Michigan, have focused on A type characteristics as a central personality measure in many of their studies. Sales (1968) developed a 49-item questionnaire test of Type A; a 9-item rationalization is now also available (Vickers, 1973). Using the Sales version, Caplan et al. (1975) found no significant correlations between personality "pure" and the "strains" measured (job dissatisfaction, somatic complaints, anxiety, depression, irritation, physical and behavioral stress correlates). Their expectation to find relationships at interactive levels, instead, is borne out by previous research experience. Caplan and Jones (1975), for example, report on the mediating role of personality. In their study of 73 male users of a university computer system in a stressful time before a 23-day shutdown, they found confirmation of previous findings that role ambiguity was positively associated with anxiety, depression and resentment, and work load with anxiety, and that these relationships were greatest for Type A personalities.

In a further study Caplan, Cobb and French (1975) investigated the relationship between smoking and A type personality and shed light on A's ability to modify his coronary-prone behavior. The team reports that only a fifth of those who try to give up smoking are successful. Following a questionnaire survey of 200 administrators, engineers and scientists at NASA, they tried to relate quitting to job stress, personality and social support. They found that quitters had the lowest levels on quantitative work load, responsibility and social support and that they scored low on Type A characteristics. Care must be taken in interpreting these correlational results (it may well be that Type As seek out high work loads). One conclusion can, however, be drawn unequivocally: Type A personalities are less likely to give up smoking than are B types (as the authors point out, over time this will lead to an increase in the association between smoking and the risk of CHD); thus it would appear that the former's characteristics are so fundamental that they are unable to help themselves (if helped they must be). Payne (1975) has this in mind when he expresses the need (in somewhat rarefied tones) for a social system of trust and support which would "manipulate the degree of environmental pressures so as to give a pinprick to the comfortable B types and respite to the harassed As."

Further confirmation of the legitimacy of the behavior pattern approach comes from the two final studies to be mentioned here. The first started from a more basic level than that above by taking a checklist of 25 habits of nervous tension (Thomas and Ross, 1963). The 1,085 medical student subjects were asked to indicate which of these corresponded to their reactions when in situations of undue pressure or stress. While highly individual patterns of response were found, it was possible to

1. Derive 8 factors (by factor analysis) from the total
    25 items—activity, appetite, irritation, visceral
    reaction, general stress, dependency, compul-
    sivity and stimulation—and suggest dimensions on
    which to base further research.
2. Relate individual items to serum cholesterol levels
    —5 items were significantly different for high and
    low cholesterol groups. Low cholesterol subjects
    more often reported loss of appetite, exhaustion,
    nausea and anxiety, and high cholesterol subjects,
    the urge to eat.

The second study is much more assumptive in approach. Gemill and Heister (1972) set out to investigate
the relationship between Machiavellianism (a tendency to
manipulate and persuade others, to initiate and control in
group situations and generally be a winner), job strain, job
satisfaction, positional mobility and perceived opportunities for formal control. High Machiavellian scorers were,
overall, much less happy in their jobs—showing more job
strain, less satisfaction and lower perceived opportunities
for formal control—than low scorers. Explanation of these
results is not easy (largely because the researchers failed
to reach the underlying elements in a complex situation).
These differences could be (1) perceptual, due to a basic
Machiavellian cynicism, (2) because of the subjects' ways
of operating which are likely to cause frustration or (3)
because they worked for formalized organizations and
not in the ambiguous environments in which they flour-
ish.

To summarize, while psychometric measures do

show relationships with stress measures, the macro approach of behavior patterns offers more practically applicable data. The doubtful reliability of psychometric tests also makes their use in causal research less intuitively appealing than that of behavioral measures.

A research technique which stands somewhat alone by explicitly incorporating personal characteristics into job stress measures (and, at the same time, reducing the number of variables in, and therefore the complexity of, multivariate analysis) is discussed by Van Harrison (1975) and French (1973). They assess person-environment fit by asking subjects to indicate desired and actual levels of work load, work complexity, responsibility, ambiguity, etc., in their jobs and then taking the difference between scores on the various dimensions as their measures. (Some other questionnaires do contain this evaluative element implicitly.) This approach has been relatively successful, and P : E fit has proved to be an equally good or more powerful predictor of stress (job dissatisfaction, anxiety, depression, etc.) than either elements separately (although there are still some unsolved problems of analysis).

3

MANAGER AND WORK: ENVIRONMENT FIT MODEL

In this chapter we shall draw on several of the themes already introduced to breathe life into the description of managerial stress. So far we have generated, separately, both the framework and the elements for a general model; it is now time to amalgamate these, look more closely at them and apply them to specific situations. In chapter 1 a theoretical model which takes into account the crucial interaction of person with environment—P : E fit—was described. Chapter 2 has now served to identify the elements, the characteristics of the individual and his job environment which are potential causes of stress (along with some of its agreed manifestations) in terms of which the model must be elaborated if it is to be specifically applied to managerial job stress. Figure 3.1 locates these elements in the general framework.

Some writers would prefer to distinguish immediate stressors from contextual environmental factors (e.g., McLean, 1976). In practice, however, this cannot be done in advance of the model's application to a particular stress situation. Even those job aspects which seem intuitively to be of relatively low priority—for the highly motivated manager, his physical working conditions, for example—may become critical in certain circumstances. On a bad day his bare, grimy office may be the last depressing pressure which renders the manager unable to cope. The same is true for the person-related variables: in one situation it may be the manager's emotional inability to accept change which puts him under stress, in another it may be his physical inability to stand up to extensive foreign travel. It is only, then, by applying the P : E fit model to a particular individual in a particular situation at a particular point in time that we can select out these dimensions of direct importance from the total universe of potentially contributing elements. Before going on to do this we would, however, like to look a little more closely at some of the finer points of this initially simple model as it is filled out here in managerial job stress terms. Two factors must be considered as a necessary background to later discussion:

1. *The nature of the job areas identified as potential stressors.* On examining the job areas included as environmental elements, three things become obvious:

1. Almost everything in the work environment is at sometime, or by someone, identified as a cause of stress.
2. Frequently, both a situation and its direct opposite can cause stress—having too much work to do *and* too little, too many decisions to make *and* too few.
3. Many of the factors quoted have been identified in

Figure 3.1 The P:E fit framework applied to managerial stress: elements found to be associated with stress

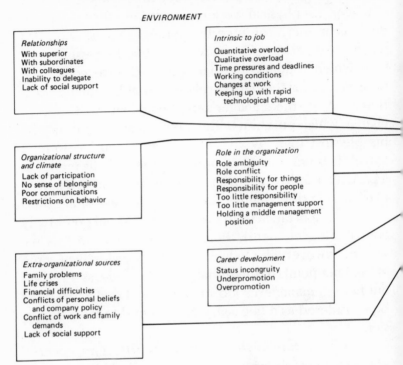

ENVIRONMENT

Relationships
With superior
With subordinates
With colleagues
Inability to delegate
Lack of social support

Intrinsic to job
Quantitative overload
Qualitative overload
Time pressures and deadlines
Working conditions
Changes at work
Keeping up with rapid
  technological change

*Organizational structure
and climate*
Lack of participation
No sense of belonging
Poor communications
Restrictions on behavior

Role in the organization
Role ambiguity
Role conflict
Responsibility for things
Responsibility for people
Too little responsibility
Too little management support
Holding a middle management
  position

Extra-organizational sources
Family problems
Life crises
Financial difficulties
Conflicts of personal beliefs
  and company policy
Conflict of work and family
  demands
Lack of social support

Career development
Status incongruity
Underpromotion
Overpromotion

other studies as direct or indirect sources of job satisfaction, e.g., a poorly defined task while causing anxiety can also provide scope for the employee to use his initiative and gain satisfaction from a job well done.

Observations (1) and (2) confirm the earlier conclusion (in chapter 1) that stress is essentially individually defined; in line with this, the second, more practically

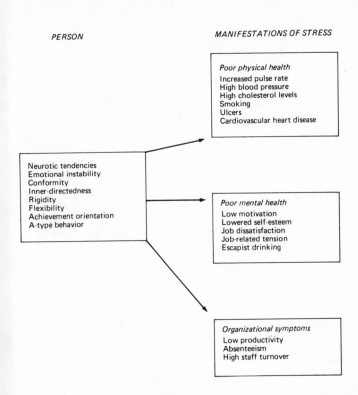

PERSON

MANIFESTATIONS OF STRESS

Poor physical health
Increased pulse rate
High blood pressure
High cholesterol levels
Smoking
Ulcers
Cardiovascular heart disease

Neurotic tendencies
Emotional instability
Conformity
Inner-directedness
Rigidity
Flexibility
Achievement orientation
A-type behavior

Poor mental health
Low motivation
Lowered self-esteem
Job dissatisfaction
Job-related tension
Escapist drinking

Organizational symptoms
Low productivity
Absenteeism
High staff turnover

oriented half of this chapter goes on to select those variables appropriate to particular groups of individuals with like characteristics performing similar job functions. It is the third point which requires further elaboration and consideration here. As stated it contradicts the suggestion implicit in much of the literature that job stress and job satisfaction are separable and usually separate experiences. Researchers typically study either one or the other and coordinate the two concepts only to make the assumption that job dissatisfaction is admissible as a measure of stress (e.g., Caplan et al., 1975), i.e., that they are opposite poles of a single continuum.

In practice it is more realistic to consider the two as parallel continua, thus adding to the already implicit axis of positive versus negative affect, that of activation level. This new conceptualization is depicted in Figure 3.2. Satisfaction in the popular sense of the word implies a relatively low, restful level of activation—Roget (1966) associates it with contentment, complacency, serenity. Managers using it to refer to aspects of their jobs appear to be using it more to mean stimulation than peace and tranquility. Looked at physiologically, too, we find support for the model: enjoyment is a state of elevated activation very similar to that identified in other contexts as one of stress (Froberg, Karlsson, Levi and Lidberg, 1967; Mills, 1976). This problem with terminology has been recognized by earlier writers and led Bernard (1968) to propose that we should differentiate linguistically between "dystress" meaning an unpleasant high activation level and "eustress" denoting one that is enjoyable. For the purposes of this book such sophistication is unnecessary; it is, however, important to note that no researchers have yet shown with conviction that it is the effect rather than the level of activation involved in the stress reaction which causes harm.

Turning to a further facet of the stress : satisfaction relationship, we have already established that pressure can contribute to feelings of satisfaction. This may be in the long run or even in the short run, if the manager is ambivalent about a particular facet of his job (Marshall,

Figure 3.2 The relationship between so-called stress and satisfaction

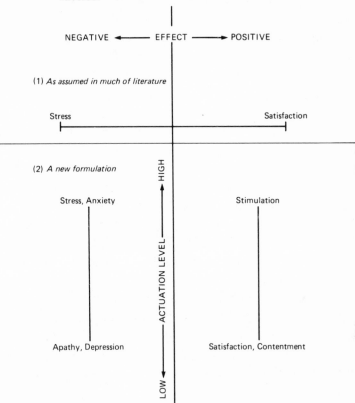

1977). In the same way job satisfaction may contribute to
job stress, either, by acting as a balance, to alleviate or,
even, to accentuate it. This last suggestion requires, perhaps, illustration. A manager who enjoys one aspect of his
job (solving technical problems, for example) may neglect
another (management of people); taking a comprehensive

59

statistical approach we would find that, for him, job satisfaction and stress from relationships are highly significantly correlated. Similarly, deriving satisfaction from his
job may lead a manager to put too much into it at the risk
of adversely affecting his general health. While we do not
wish to labor this point, it is important, then, to bear in
mind the interdependence of the positive and negative
dimensions of experience.

If we can understand the interaction and relative
contribution of good and bad environmental factors to the
causation of stress, we not only achieve a more comprehensive picture of the real world but also have more
power when we come to apply our results in it. A justifia-
ble retort of higher management called on to eliminate
potential stressors from the workplace is that they are
beneficial (a) to the organization as an impetus to growth
and survival and (b) to the individual as direct and indirect
sources of achievement and satisfaction. If we, as researchers and possible stimulators of change, can con-
vince them that there are ways of identifying harmful
stress and remedying this *alone,* we have more chance of
being heard and of helping, rather than damaging, the
organization.

2. *The necessity of considering both contributing systems.* The P:E fit model assumes that a knowledge of
both systems and their interaction is necessary to a full
understanding of the causation of stress. While this is true
in the majority of cases, the possibility that one or another
"actor" will dominate in specific circumstances is not excluded. There are some individuals who seem by nature
to be excessively vulnerable and who have difficulty cop-

ing with even relatively mundane tasks; for them person-related variables will always dominate the stress equation. In other situations the environment appears to be almost wholly to blame. Certain jobs or certain working environments seem to be intrinsically stressful and to have harmful effects no matter how initially immune the incumbent is. Research suggests, for example, that middle management positions make so many exacting demands that their occupants run an abnormally high risk of developing symptoms of stress (Kay, 1974). It is commonly believed that the salesman, too, is in an intrinsically difficult situation: "The people in the company who are most afraid of most people are the salesmen. They live and work under pressure that is extraordinary . . . when things are bad, they are worse for the salesmen; when things are good, they are not much better" (Heller, 1975). It is, nonetheless, important to treat the development of stress as a *potentially* two-sided affair, and we shall continue to do so in the second half of this chapter, even though simpler explanations may sometimes be adequate.

PRACTICAL APPLICATION OF THE P:E FIT MODEL

In Figure 3.1 we have, then, the general model of managerial stress, an awesome list of potential environmental stressors and individual weaknesses. We shall now go on to make use of it by treating its elements as a pool from which to draw those relevant to particular circumstances. Three levels of analysis are open to us;

here we have chosen the intermediate course. We could look at an individual case study, assessing from interview and/or questionnaire material what the manager's job pressures and vulnerabilities are and depicting them in P:E fit terms. This is the approach adopted by a counselor (the manager's wife, doctor or personnel officer, for example) and by the more anecdotal, company doctor type writers in the stress field (e.g., Brook, 1973). It is, however, of limited generality and would have, in this context, to be fictitious. At the other extreme, we could look for a general, population-wide stress prediction equation. Research suggests that, even if this is statistically possible, it is too general to be of any practical use (Marshall, 1977) and the theoretical points made under (1) above cast doubts on its conceptual desirability. We have, then, decided on an approach midway between the two—to look for and apply the P:E fit model to meaningful subgroups within the managerial population. Here we shall segment managers according to job function as this appears to be the most significant discriminating variable. Our aim is to pick out from the pool of potential stressors those relevant to a particular group. Appley and Trumbull (1967) have used the phrase "vulnerability profile" to refer to the person half of the picture thus derived; here we shall extend their terminology to include environmental variables predictive of stress in so-called stress profiles. Each multivariable description presented is, then, that of an individual at risk. The profiles presented below are drawn from a variety of sources. They vary particularly as to the criteria of stress used—subjective report, objective measure such as incidence of cardiovascular heart disease or the writers' observation and intuition—and the extent to which they include the less accessible person-related variables in the stress prediction equation. (Some nonmanagerial groups are included where relevant.) In our treatment, we shall deal in turn with job environment-dominated and person-dominated descriptions before turning to more recent research which has made a conscious effort to view the two systems simultaneously.

The first profile we should like to consider, while not that of a management group and only sketchily drawn, is a good illustration of the futility of trying to treat contributing elements in isolation. In a study of cardiovascular heart disease among bus drivers and conductors, Morris (1953) tried to assess the relative importance of two main differentiating variables: inactivity and job stress. He found that while, overall, conductors have a lower incidence of disease than drivers (suggesting that inactivity is the greater risk factor), city crews had a higher incidence of disease than their suburban counterparts (leading him to conclude that job stress is, in fact, the more important). A more recently proposed explanation of the results is that exposure to exhaust fumes accounts for the different rates of disease. That the academic debate as to the chief cause should continue for so long is rather disheartening since the various contributing factors are part of a general life-style, are probably interactive and cannot be separated out for study. In the remainder of this chapter we shall, therefore, try to avoid the trap of trying to identify the one cause of stress for a

63

particular group and shall, rather, adopt a profile approach.

An occupational group which has taken a notable lead in investigating and taking action to prevent its own job stress are air traffic controllers. Members have been most willing to take part in research, organize symposiums on stress and cooperate with the relevant authorities in carefully controlling and monitoring their working procedures and fitness for duty. Theirs is an example of a job which has a relatively high number of intrinsically stressful components: responsibility for the lives of large numbers of people, having to make decisions quickly and accurately, maintaining concentration over long periods of time and working unsocial hours, but which its incumbents find highly satisfying as well as stressful (Manchester, 1976). Working from intuitive evidence, we should expect these factors to dominate the environment side of the ATC's stress profile. We must, however, beware of judging *from the outside* what a particular job incumbent finds stressful—"One man's stress is another man's challenge" (McGrath, 1970c). The observer, biased as he is by his own motivations, can completely misjudge the situation, seeing as stressful those elements for which the individual concerned actually chose the job. It is, therefore, more valuable to have the subjects' self-assessment or some objective measure of harm as a criterion. If we listen to the air traffic controllers' complaints about their jobs, we find a rather different pattern. Their concerns appear to be less global, less high-minded, and having more to do with everyday operating conditions than those listed above. Maxwell (1976) confirms only one of our preconceived pressures—the number of hours on duty without a break—adding to it fluctuations in work load, poor working conditions (reflection from instruments, seat design, etc.), interpersonal problems (particularly with higher management), fear of losing one's license by failing the strict, regular medical examination and fear of loss of picture (a temporary amnesia which prevents the ATC from fitting all the vital details together meaningfully). Presumably, person variables—an aptitude for, and training in, making the complex decisions required, long familiarity with responsibility, etc.—have intervened to turn some potential stressors into neutral characteristics of the job or even satisfactions.

Turning now to managerial populations, we find that while much has been written on the topic, there is little specific enough to suit our purposes. We must, therefore, rely more on our interpretation, than on direct statements, of findings.

Kahn et al. (1964) concentrated, in their seminal research, on the two related job pressures: role conflict and role ambiguity. While these are likely to affect most job holders at some time, they suggest that they are almost written into the job descriptions of those at organizational boundaries. Wind (1971), from data collected in a study of industrial buying behavior, illustrates this by describing the conflicts facing the purchasing officer within a company. In buying components he must try to satisfy the R & D engineer's high technical specifications, the production function's needs for continuous supply and the chief accountant's objectives of minimum cost. As a way of avoiding some of the potential stress in his job, Wind

65

found that the purchasing officer would favor whichever of these three organizational groups had the greatest control over his immediate rewards. This varied with organizational structure. In centralized companies he was more likely to include the purchasing department in his loyalty domain and in decentralized companies to cater to the engineers with whom he was in direct personal contact.

So far we have concentrated on identifying the environmental factors which make a particular job stressful; we also know that, given a certain set of demands, some people perform relatively more successfully than do others. We may speculate about the key to their success, but we can also approach the person side of the equation more systematically and try to ascertain what characteristics make individuals more or less vulnerable to external pressure. Age, sex, physique, manual aptitude, educational attainment are all potentially important here and have long been used as bases for personnel selection. A more interesting dimension, as far as the psychologist is concerned, and one whose action is less well understood, is personality. Two questions are relevant here: the first is whether the individual's personality profile is suitable for a particular job, and the second whether he is, at a general level, vulnerable to pressure.

Research carried out by Hartston and Mottram (1975) is relevant to the first question and offers reassuring results for most of the managerial job functions studied. Using Cattell's 16 Personality Factor test, they compared the scores of 603 middle managers to population norms and looked for differences between the various functions represented. It is the second analysis which is of interest here. Rather than being able to identify groups at risk of stress, though, we find that most have personality profiles which seem eminently well suited to the jobs they do. Bank managers were people oriented, more conservative and conscientious than the norm; accountants were precise and objective; salesmen outgoing, adaptable and competitive. Only two functions showed obvious signs of vulnerability and that only when the wider implications of their roles as managers were considered. Engineers emerged as critical and aloof, introspective, realistic, nononsense people, conventional and practical; research and development managers as critical, brighter than the already high norm, realistic but restrained and inhibited. Both profiles are suggestive of employees who will be competent at their primary functions, but ill equipped to cope with, and unsympathetic toward, peripheral interpersonal demands. Such faults will greatly reduce their suitability for promotion to higher, task-free, managerial positions. Hartston and Mottram's results suggest (albeit tentatively) that in most managerial functions it is the individual whose personality deviates from the norm who is at risk of showing stress symptoms because of demands intrinsic to the job.

The most significant work relating to the second question is that of Friedman and Rosenman at San Francisco Medical Center already described in detail in chapter 2. Not only is the A type personality more vulnerable to external pressure than his B type colleague, but he also appears to be stress seeking and to be less able to adopt the adaptive coping strategies available to him.

Looking at personality alone is again, however, to

focus on only one half of a pair of interacting systems. Using modern statistical techniques, such as multiple regression and cluster analysis (e.g., Kecka, Nie and Hull, 1975), researchers now have the facility to handle and make sense of large numbers of interacting variables simultaneously. Such an intention motivated the latest study by the Institute of Social Research at Michigan (Caplan et al., 1975). They include a wide range of variables thought to be causally related to strain (any deviation from normal responses in the person)—health-related behaviors (smoking, diet, etc.), personality, subjective environment (quantitative and qualitative work load, responsibility for people and for things, job complexity, role conflict, participation, etc.) and person : environment fit on four job dimensions. Their first report deals mainly with univariate analyses, but already evidence is emerging of two distinctive clusters of stressful job conditions (they have taken as their sample 2,010 employees in 23 different occupational groups preselected as being highly stressful, but avoiding physical hazards, and ranging from factory workers to administrative professors). These are:

1. Low utilization of abilities, low participation, low work complexity and poor person : environment fit—exemplified by assembly line workers
2. High quantitative work load, a need for sustained concentration, and high responsibility for people —these were typical of administrative professors and physicians who also scored highest on a measure of coronary-prone personality

In recent papers they draw more differentiated conclusions. They find, for example, that work overload leads to job dissatisfaction for all the occupational groups studied; underload, on the other hand, was so related for scientists and administrators (i.e., those who valued high job complexity) but not for policemen and assembly line workers (Van Harrison, 1975).

Kahn et al. (1964), too, have something to say about the differential interaction of personality with environmental factors. They found, for example, that the stress situation develops differently for the introverted than for the extroverted personality. Under stress from role conflict, the former tends to reduce his contacts with other people. His defensive withdrawal only serves to aggravate the situation: his role senders see this as being overly independent and react by intensifying their attempts to influence him, putting him under increased interpersonal pressure. His coping strategy is, therefore, self-defeating. The extrovert, on the other hand, does not show the extremes of interpersonal tension in which such behavior typically results. He is not as vulnerable to role conflict as the introvert and, anyway, reacts more openly and adaptively if it does arise. Kahn et al. also found differences between rigid and flexible personalities both in the type of situation they perceived as stressful and in the nature and range of coping strategies they used. In this differentiation it is less easy to assess which personality type is acting the more constructively. The rigid personality tends to avoid conflict and tension by rejecting disruptive environmental inputs (and the role senders from whom they come), showing increased dependence on authority figures and falling back on compulsive work habits. In so doing he avoids immediate stress but removes himself from reality and adds further restrictions to an already restricted life. The flexible personality shows more varied responses to pressure in which the researchers saw two underlying themes: compliance to environmental demands, and a tendency to seek help from peers and subordinates. While these can have beneficial outcomes there are obvious drawbacks in both techniques: they encourage overload (and shifting personal values), and do not involve those most able to help (one's superior role senders), respectively. Extrapolating from results such as these, we can suggest that different personality types will be more suited than others to fill particular jobs. The role-conflict susceptible introvert will be particularly at risk in an organizational boundary position, the rigid personality in one which requires him to cope adaptively with a fast-changing environment, for example.

So far we have substantiated, but illustrated only sketchily, the claim that distinctive patterns of interacting person and environment variables cause stress; in the final section of this chapter we shall look more closely at the research-based stress profiles of five managerial job functions. The study from which the data was taken (Marshall, 1977) was designed specifically to operationalize the P : E fit model. The individuals at risk described here were arrived at via multiple regression analyses and did not necessarily exist within the sample of 200 senior managers studied (one might say that they are figments of the computer's imagination), but if they had done so they would have been very likely to achieve high scores on the physical and psychological criteria of stress used. Allowing for the weaknesses of the available correlational statistical techniques as a basis for causal inference (see chapter 8) and the small sample sizes for certain functions, and supplementing empirical with qualitative research data, the aim below will be to catch the gestalt of each profile rather than pay close attention to detail. (For each profile a P: E fit equation tabulates those elements found to be associated with high scores on the psychological and physiological stress criteria measures used in the study.)

Figure 3.3
STRESS PROFILE OF THE RESEARCH MANAGER

Environmental elements	Person-related elements
Manages people (reported as a satisfaction)*	Is independent, assertive (and less bright than others in the department)
Works for a large company (satisfaction)	Older
	Less career mobility than colleagues
	Looks outside work for satisfaction

*Unless otherwise stated, environmental stressors were reported by respondents as being pressures (rather than satisfactions).

The *research manager* (Figure 3.3) at risk of showing symptoms of stress is older than others in his department but has less experience in terms of movement within the company. His personality profile is that of an assertive, controlled, self-sufficient individual who is possibly less bright than his colleagues. (The measure of intelligence used in the study is too superficial to be treated very seriously; the variable, therefore, appears in brackets in the figures.) He reports deriving satisfaction from managing people and from working for the company, but as these areas contribute to high scores on the stress criteria measures, we must conclude that he does not find these particular aspects of his job easy; they are, it seems, in conflict with his personality and (lack of) past experience. His diversion of time and commitment to activities outside work (to which he looks for satisfaction) is likely to put him under additional pressure. Overall, this is the picture of a manager whose needs and abilities, while appropriate to his main function, do not match the demands (of managing people and feeling at ease working in a large organization) inherent in his job; we might say that there is "poor fit" between him and his immediate environment. (The results of Hartston and Mottram mentioned earlier suggest that this is a common risk for individuals in such functions.) It is unlikely that he will be called on to change at this stage in his career, and his apparent orientation outside the company may well be a way of achieving a new balance between the various areas of his life.

Within the *production function* two distinctive stress profiles were revealed—one, the more active pattern, being associated with psychological symptoms of stress (anxiety), the other, a comparatively passive cluster, with poorer scores on a physical health scale (Figures 3.4 and 3.5, respectively).

Environmental variables dominate the explanation

Figure 3.4

STRESS PROFILE OF THE PRODUCTION MANAGER:
P : E COMBINATION PREDICTIVE OF HIGH ANXIETY
SCORES

Environmental elements	Person-related elements
Job insecurity	Is reserved and group dependent
Works for a large company (satisfaction)	Less career mobility than colleagues
Lacks autonomy	
Quantitative overload	
Qualitative overload (satisfaction)	

Figure 3.5

STRESS PROFILE OF THE PRODUCTION MANAGER:
P : E COMBINATION PREDICTIVE OF POOR PHYSICAL
HEALTH SCORES

Environmental elements	Person-related elements
No significant contributors	Is sensitive (and less bright than others in the group)
	Older
	Lower managerial level
	Has a nonworking wife

of higher anxiety scores. Three themes emerge in the list of factors the production manager at risk reports as pressures:

1. Lack of job security
2. Occupying an overloading and challenging job
3. Feelings of frustration at belonging to a large company and the lack of autonomy this involves

73

The production manager works in a situation of constant demand. His job is both quantitatively and qualitatively overloading, but, typically, he enjoys and derives direct and indirect satisfaction from mastering its challenges. The manager at risk is, however, not in the position to make the most of such opportunities for achievement as he is under additional pressure from two directions. Firstly, there is the pressure from above, from geographically distant higher management who make decisions with which he may not agree but which he has to implement. (His doubts about his job security are a further indication of the poor quality of this relationship.) Secondly, today's production manager feels his autonomy threatened from below. Greater participation for blue collar and junior white collar workers is severely eroding his power and authority within the organization. If we add in, finally, the personality dimensions predictive of psychological symptoms of stress—tendencies to be reserved and group dependent—we see an individual who may well be reluctant to assert himself in this situation.

In direct contrast, the production manager at risk of showing *physical* symptoms of stress is not under obvious pressure from his current job. He is, rather, the victim of a lack of achievement in the past, being older but at a lower managerial level than his colleagues. His profile shows signs of emotional vulnerability (a tendency to worry); whether or not this has helped to cause his career frustration, it is likely to make him react badly to failure. The manager's wife is unlikely to work full time which suggests that she too relies on his success for life satisfaction, thus putting him under added pressure to achieve.

The manager in this situation may well find accepting and adjusting to having reached his career ceiling difficult, especially if he feels that he must hide his disappointment from his wife.

Figure 3.6
STRESS PROFILE OF THE SERVICE MANAGER

Environmental elements	*Person-related elements*
Lacking autonomy	Is ambitious and anxiety prone
Works for a large company (satisfaction)	
Has been recently promoted	
Has been longer than colleagues in the same location	

For the purposes of analysis several small function groups were amalgamated and classed as *service managers* (Figure 3.6). This category included people such as accountants, patents and personnel officers, performing rather different functions but with similar relationships to the rest of the organization. The researcher's inability to find any immediate job elements of significance to the manager at risk is probably an indication of meaningful variations in job demands between the group's constituent elements. The environmental factors associated with stress for this group all reflect feelings of a lack of autonomy and authority. It would seem that for the manager at risk the service role, having expert knowledge but being in an advisory rather than a directly participating position when decisions are being made, was a source of frustration. Viewed in the context of the personality characteristics which contribute to higher stress scores—a tendency to anxiety twinned with ambition—the problem his organization role presents is even more readily understandable. Again it would appear that the manager's wife is likely to be at least financially, if not emotionally, dependent on his career success—another incentive/pressure for him to do well. Having been recently promoted has not served to improve his feelings of independence (we shall suggest in chapter 4 that it is a mistake to think that top management have boundless power); in fact, it would appear that becoming more involved with (and dependent on) the company has served to accentuate this employee's powerlessness. In both its person and environment components this profile bears a striking resemblance to that of the dissatisfied Machiavellian manager described by Gemill and Heisler (1972) and referred to in chapter 2. It suggests that ambition and a high need for independence are dangerous characteristics for the service manager in a large company especially if he is, by nature, prone to anxiety.

Figure 3.7

STRESS PROFILE OF THE MARKETING MANAGER

Environmental elements	Person-related elements
Quantitative overload	Is ambitious, anxiety prone and introverted
Qualitative overload	Looks outside work for satisfaction

The *marketing manager* (Figure 3.7) at risk is very similar in character to his service department colleague—

he too shows considerable evidence of being anxiety prone, combining this with ambition; his job situation is, however, markedly different. For him the main problem is work overload and he reports both too much to do and too many challenges in his job. As with the researcher there is a suggestion that looking outside work for satisfaction may be reducing the manager's ability to cope with what seems to be a highly demanding position. This is, possibly, the profile of an individual who has been over-promoted, since there is no evidence, as there was for the service manager, that his job demands have recently peaked.

With the same vulnerable personality profile, these two managers find themselves in objectively very different but, in terms of their resulting experiences of stress, very similar situations. The first (the service manager) has chosen a combination of speciality and size of company in which his needs are unlikely to be met; the second (the marketing manager) has let his needs outrun his capabilities to such an extent that he is in danger.

Figure 3.8
STRESS PROFILE OF THE ENGINEERING MANAGER

Environmental elements	*Person-related elements*
Job insecurity	Is practical, anxiety prone (and less bright than others in the department)
Lacks autonomy	Older
Quantitative overload (satisfaction)	Lower managerial level
	Looks outside work for satisfaction

The most surprising characteristic of the last stress profile, that of the *engineering manager* (Figure 3.8), is the prominence of reported satisfaction from job challenges. It is only when we view this element in the context of the remaining job factors in the pattern that this becomes understandable. The engineer at risk shows several symptoms of being dissatisfied with his career progress: he is older but at a lower managerial level than his colleagues in the department, feels that he lacks autonomy and is also unsure about his future job security. This suggests that he does not have the power and authority to perform as he would like, no matter what opportunities he feels there are for achievement. His personality profile suggests that he is unlikely to cope easily with such a situation of perceived external constraint, he is practical but sensitive and worrying. This manager, too, looks outside work for satisfaction, but in his case it is likely to be an attempt to compensate for reduced job involvement rather than a competitive drain on his energies. Several factors may be at work here. This profile, more than any other, suggests a group whose situation has been worsened (perhaps largely caused) by the economic climate at the time of data collection (1974–5). Engineering departments exist within companies to spend money and are among the first to suffer from cutbacks in capital expenditure during a recession. The feeling of being undervalued permeates this profile.

We see from these analyses that while the universe of potential stressors is vast, for any group of individuals with common characteristics it can be reduced to a manageable number of critical dimensions. The above profiles are valuable, then, firstly for their content: they provide a sufficiently detailed picture to form the basis of considered action at a group level and also reveal repeated themes (lack of autonomy, career development problems, for example) which suggest pressures of more general relevance. Secondly, they have methodological implications, suggesting that diagnosis of stress within an organization (assuming realistically that one cannot cater to the specific needs of each and every employee) should be at the level of distinguishable subgroups rather than that of the general organizational member. In so doing they cast doubt on the usefulness of studies which seek to treat management as an undifferentiated group.

4

ORGANIZATIONAL MEMBERSHIP AS A SOURCE OF STRESS: ITS EFFECTS ON THE MIDDLE MANAGER AND THE MIDDLE-AGED

Chapter 3 emphasized the individual's specific nature of stress definition and focused on the manager as the performer of a particular job function. Several of its themes, however, had little to do with the type of work he does and were more relevant to the manager in his general role as an organizational member. It is these wider aspects of the manager's work life, his relationships with the organization and its other members, which we would now like to consider in more depth. Organizational membership appears as a pressure in two closely related ways: in the restrictions it places on the individual's day-to-day activities and in the control it exercises over his future development. These will be discussed in turn; in the first section a further distinction between pressures which have long been acknowledged and those which are the result of more recent trends in society can also be made.

DAY-TO-DAY RESTRICTIONS

By locating the individual in a particular management position, the organization makes him vulnerable to two, almost classic, work pressures identified in the literature—role ambiguity and role conflict (Kahn et al.). These will not, however, be further elaborated at this particular point, firstly, because they have already been introduced and described in broad terms in chapter 2 and, secondly, because many of the topics covered in the rest of this chapter are really little more than illustrations of these two general themes. A second way in which organizational membership can be a source of pressure is by the limits it sets to the individual's freedom of action. In return for the pay and the wide range of opportunities they offer, organizations make certain basic demands of their employees. In time most people come to accept that they should spend the hours between 9 and 5, Monday to Friday, at work, abiding by the organization's rules, dressing appropriately, and while there, occupying themselves with tasks imposed on them, with varying degrees of supervision, from outside. Conditions in excess of these basic requirements vary from job to job; a typical manager, when asked, will also categorize working unpaid overtime and attending work-related social events as part of the job. For almost all employees such requirements are a source of irritation at some time, but it is a minority who find them such an intolerable burden that they must opt out altogether. Some restrictions along these lines are, in fact, essential if a company is to function efficiently. They provide an understandable and predictable struc-

81

ture within which employees can work. Variations on the structure may be possible—many firms are now introducing flexible working hours, for example—but only outside certain necessary bounds. Most companies insist that certain core hours, usually 10 to 12 and 2 to 4, are observed by all to facilitate contact between departments and with other companies.

Control of an employee's behavior is not, however, always to the company's good; in some cases it may even interfere with the former's ability to do his job well. If the individual always has to check back with higher management, often along a chain of command several links long, before making a decision, this can, for example, considerably slow his and, therefore, the organization's ability to react to and cope with a changing environment. The procedures involved, as well as the time they take, can be a source of frustration for the individual concerned. The scope for independent action in a given job (often measured by the incumbent's jurisdiction over expenditure—his signing ability—or his power to arrive late for work) is an important sign of its worth/desirability. A frequent complaint of today's manager is that he has responsibility, but not authority; whichever way he looks he finds that his ability to act autonomously is being eroded. This is most noticeable, and most painful, in relation to his power to make decisions. The average manager is having to confer with and seek the approval of more and more people in his decision making. An initial move in this direction was the trend to decision making by committee, a sensible measure designed to ensure that important decisions are not made wantonly. For the individual manager it can, however, be a considerable source of pressure; he must elicit the agreement of all his fellow members, even those who are unreasonable or plainly ignorant in a topic area, before he can proceed with a proposed course of action. Parkinson (1957) points to some of the problems of decision making by committee and is persuasive in his argument that devoting only two and a half minutes to planning a $10 million atomic reactor but forty-five to a proposed new bicycle shed is understandable. In such situations it may be that the most powerful politician wins or that a good plan is made ineffective by compromise; participating in such games can be stressful as well as time consuming. Having to supplement one of (say) eight votes with power and influence in order to affect policy making can, then, be taxing, but the manager does have opportunities for success; having no say in decision making at all can be even more frustrating. The role of many specialist managers, company accountants, for example, is to act in an advisory capacity only, having no official right to do more than express an opinion. As organizations become larger and the environments they deal with more complex, an increasing number of managers are likely to find themselves in such positions, at the periphery of the main action in the company. Alienation is the sociologists' word for the feeling of being a disposable number to which this can lead; Heller (1975) describes it in the following terms:

> What would happen, if deliberately, calmly, with malice, aforethought and obvious premeditation, I disobeyed?
> I know what would happen: nothing. Nothing

would happen. And the knowledge depresses me . . .

I suppose it is just about impossible for someone like me to rebel anymore and produce any kind of lasting effect. I have lost the power to upset things that I had as a child; I can no longer change my environment or even disturb it seriously. They would simply fire and forget me as soon as I tried.

Levinson (1973) suggests that the specialists' role is problematic not only to them but also to the decision makers whom they advise. He talks of the manager's dependence on specialists, whom he cannot understand or control, as being an important source of pressure.

Whether or not he has a say in decision making, the typical manager will find himself at some time having to implement policies with which he does not agree. This is likely to be one of the more difficult constraints of company membership with which he has to cope. Personal characteristics and his overall situation will play a large part in determining the individual manager's reaction to this conflict between his organizational and private roles. His so-called tolerance of ambiguity (Budner, 1962) may well be an important factor here. One way of avoiding the conflict altogether is for the manager to have no opinion of his own in the first place. The all-powerful C.J., for example, has learned to expect this from his staff (Nobbs, 1975):

"But I don't say to you: 'Pull your socks up, Reggie.' I say to you: 'Overall sales, across the whole spectrum, were down 0.1 per cent in April.' I leave you to draw your own conclusions—and pull your socks up."

"Yes, C.J."

"I didn't get where I am today without learning how to handle people."

"No, C.J."

"I give them a warning shot across the bows, but I don't let them realize that I'm giving them a warning shot across the bows."

"Yes, C.J."

"Not that I want to be entirely surrounded by yes-men."

"No, C.J."

Reggie's behavioral compliance is not, however, as wholehearted as his verbal agreement! Company practice, but particularly one's immediate superior's technique, has an important role to play here. Writers suggest that good communications, by informing the manager of the reasons behind unpalatable decisions, can go a long way towards eliciting his active cooperation (e.g. Golembiewski and McConkie, 1975). It also appears that if an employee has been allowed to express his opinion, and is confident that it has been heard, he will be more amenable to following the course higher management eventually dictates (Marshall, 1977). The difference between willing and unwilling implementation of policies is, perhaps, more important at managerial than at other levels of the organization. Any task, but especially those which have only been specified in global terms, can be performed better by a motivated than an unmotivated worker; in addition, the manager may well fail in his primary duty of selling an idea to his subordinates if he himself doubts its soundness.

The conclusion from our discussion so far is that the manager's autonomy is severely restricted from above and we see that there is a real need for greater worker participation even at this level of the organization. Setting aside for a moment how this might be achieved, a topic to which we return in chapter 7, it is important to note that we can expect beneficial outcomes at several accounting levels by such a development. Moves in this direction might not only increase individuals' immediate job satisfaction (relegating to the background any frustrations about more necessary restrictions of their liberty) and improve the quality of life within organizations, it might also help to provide a much needed fillip to the national economy. Marrow (1973) suggests that a consideration of the average annual increase in manufacturing output per man hour between 1965 and 1970 for the major non-Communist countries "comes down heavily on the side of 'the sharing of power.' " At the top of the league are Japan and The Netherlands with increases of 14.2 percent and 8.5 percent respectively, and at the bottom, the U.K. and U.S.A. with 3.6 percent and 1.9 percent.

So far we have concentrated on the manager's relationship with higher management; company membership also involves him in relationships downwards, with his subordinates. Even in normal circumstances these, too, can be a source of pressure, but the relatively recent movement toward greater worker participation and the shift of considerable amounts of power toward the blue collar workers has made them a growing cause for concern. Approval for any proposed course of action now has to be sought not only from superiors (those of like opinion) but also from the work force (whose values often differ radically). Not only has this eroded the manager's power and authority, diminishing both his status and self-esteem, it has also severely taxed his interpersonal skills. Many of today's managers were educated and later trained to expect that they would make the decisions and that their jobs would mainly involve dealing with things. The interpersonal aspects were expected, by and large, to be peripheral. When problems with people, which were once seen as trivial, take up a major part of the day, many managers have trouble deciding how best to allocate their time and many, also, find that they lack the tact necessary to cope with this new dimension to their job. If he cannot adapt his priorities accordingly, the manager may find that he is deriving less satisfaction from work than he did at earlier task-dominated stages of his career. Many of today's managers feel more threatened by the power below, than that above, them in the organization and are currently struggling to come to terms with their new role. It is impossible to say at this stage where worker : manager : higher management relationships will next stabilize; it is evident, however, that our current period of transition is a source of pressure at all three organizational levels.

Taking all the above factors together, we find that managers as a group, the supposed controllers of industry, are as potentially powerless as employees at lower levels of the company. Even very senior managers are not free (some find, with disappointment, that they are less free) to make decisions on their own. It seems likely, and research has confirmed (Kay, 1975; Margolis and Kroes, 1974; Marshall, 1977), that it is to those at middle-management levels that lack of autonomy is the greatest pressure. The middle manager is particularly likely to feel boxed-in, a feeling that a quick glance at his place on the organization chart can only act to confirm. He is distant enough from top management to have little say in policy decision making, but near enough to junior management to be a receiver of any pressure emanating from lower levels of the organization. As a link in a chain he is, by definition, vulnerable to role conflict and may well have difficulty reconciling the messages from below with those from above him. Those in the middle of an organization find it difficult to initiate action. If there is something he wishes to do, the middle manager must first seek approval from his superiors (probably several levels thereof), then coordinate his plans laterally, involving colleagues over whom he has no formal control and, finally, organize their execution downward by delegating to his subordinates. He will be extremely lucky if his initial idea is not hopelessly compromised by such formidable procedures. The further from a direct and meaningful task his job is, the more likely it becomes that there will also be ambiguities about the manager's function within the company.

Career development is likely to be particularly important to the middle manager. He has typically shown enough ambition in the past to raise himself above jobs from which he can derive direct task-based satisfaction —being an engineer or accountant, for example—and has become increasingly motivated by promotion. Opportunities for advancement are, therefore, a focus of concern and are likely to influence his relationships with superiors (he cannot make mistakes or enemies), his colleagues (his natural rivals) and his subordinates (potential rivals). Kay (1975) suggests that middle managers are more vulnerable to job insecurity and are more likely to be asked to retire early than those above or below them. He also points to pay compression as a source of pressure, as their salaries fall behind relative to those of new recruits. Within the organization middle management positions are, then, characterized by pressure from many directions and commensurately lacking in opportunities for social support. A final problem is that this may even have implications outside the company; the middle manager's ambiguous organizational position can sour his relationships with the wider community by failing to confer on him a meaningful job title and, therefore, status.

Before turning to the second main theme of this chapter, we should like to mention briefly three further forces which, though external to the company, act to restrict the individual manager's power and autonomy. The first is the now increasingly vocal consumer. Not only must the company produce acceptable, serviceable goods (the proliferation of customer service departments in the last five years is evidence that complaints about product quality are being taken increasingly seriously), it must also be seen to be socially responsible in its use of natural resources, treatment of its employees, political affiliation, etc. Profit maximization alone was a hard enough goal; the manager in his work must now balance his accounts in multidimensional space and live with the conflicts this involves. The government in its official dealings with organizational members and its private dealings with the individual is (respectively) the source of our second and third pressures. In his work the manager must comply with the constraints of a growing body of intricate legislation. At home, too, the manager has cause to feel that he is the victim of too much government attention. His financial situation, a key to his previously high status in society, is deteriorating rapidly relative to other segments of the work force (Johnson, 1976). Between 1970 and 1975 salaries of different managerial jobs suffered falls. Those of manual and nonmanual adult men, meanwhile, rose. While such movements can be argued to be fair, they are, nonetheless, painful for the middle classes who are currently being leveled down.

A symptom of managers' current dissatisfaction with their organizational and societal role is their growing interest in unionization (e.g. Johnson, 1976). Argyris (1964) sees the setting up of informal groups as a natural reaction of mature adults required to take on a childish role (i.e., one lacking opportunities for autonomy) by the organization that employs them. In eight cogently argued propositions he shows that these informal groups, and the instrumental attitude to work they foster, act to reinforce the alienating company structure from which they emanated. We are seeing his predictions fulfilled for substantial sectors of the manual work force; their validation at managerial levels too would be a particularly unwelcome development.

Figure 4.1 Pressures on the manager from his organizational membership

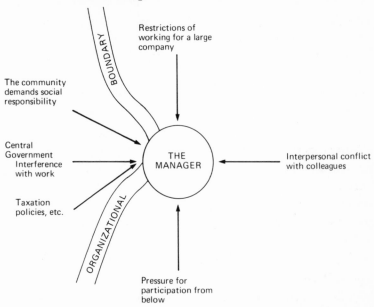

Figure 4.1 summarizes the potential stressors discussed so far in this chapter; it represents the managers at one point in time at the focus of the various forces acting on him. We shall now take a more dynamic view of his relationship with the company. The changes in company demand and employee reward to be described are summarized in Figure 7.2 of chapter 7 as an introduction to a consideration of how the individual concerned and his employing company might act to cope with the problems they often cause.

CONTROL OF THE MANAGER'S FUTURE

The company controls not only the individual's current job situation but also, over time, his career development. Managers are typically depicted as being addicted to work (but rather more for the power and status it confers than for actual job content), excessively ambitious and willing to sacrifice family, friends, conscience and health to the ultimate goal of becoming managing director, chief executive, etc. (Heller, 1975; Braine, 1962; Wilson, 1972). Many, and particularly the young ones, do, in fact, subscribe to a subset at least of these ideals, and we find that employer companies (and the society in which the latter are embedded) foster their continuation by the demands they make of, and the rewards they give, their executives.

To the young manager a company typically offers a wide, if particularized, range of experiences and opportunities. In return it expects high levels of commitment in terms of both time and energy. While he may enjoy each job he does for its own sake, the manager is usually in it only long enough to master it and is then moved on. At this stage the company is keen to expand his training by experience and his chief rewards are higher pay and promotion. The manager learns to subscribe to, and work for, this value system and may sometimes accept a job he does not want to do in an area of the country he would rather not live if it is the next step up and fits in with his long-term career aspirations. He thus becomes future-motivated, often to the detriment of the present, losing interest in performing one job as soon as the next move is planned (Marshall and Cooper, 1976a).

There are three potentially stressful strands to career development (the first being the most relevant to the individual just described) which are: competition, uncertainty and frustration. The young manager is usually striving to make his mark before it becomes too late—he appreciates that his is a young man's game. With no or little experience (acquired credits) behind him, he feels a need not only to perform well but also not to make mistakes or enemies which will later count against him. His eagerness is often reflected in working long hours and after work socializing (and politicking) to keep ahead of his contemporaries, many of whom are adopting the same tactics. Relationships with colleagues may, then, be a source of added pressure and this can be a time of considerable isolation for the young manager as he keeps his own council from both his rivals at work and his wife for whom he may have little time (Guest and Williams, 1973; Beattie, Darlington and Cripps, 1974). Uncertainty (if the company is not frank about its plans for him) and frustration (if he stays more than two to three years in any one position) may also be pressures, but at this career stage he is still relatively mobile and does not have to stay with a firm if he is dissatisfied with the rewards he is receiving. In normal times the young executive is usually quick to move to a new company to achieve the next step up, more pay, greater responsibility, better prospects, etc. (Many companies encourage and feel that they benefit from mobility in the work force; others adopt a more closed-shop approach and prefer to train and develop their employees from scratch, rewarding long service with relatively high job security and a faintly paternalistic attitude to em-

93

ployee welfare.) Any factors which act to restrict the flow of manpower between companies will increase stress from concern about career development and become pressures in their turn. An economic recession creates just such an effect and causes young managers to feel frustrated at their lack of opportunities. Other restrictions on an individual's prospects outside his present company—having little generalizable experience, feeling unable to take a risk because of one's financial commitments, his wife's refusal to move from a particular area—will all have similar effects.

Career development is then a problem to the younger manager but it also brings considerable rewards and satisfactions; even competition is not a wholly negative facet, and many actively enjoy the interpersonal and employee : company conflict characteristic of this stage (Marshall, 1977). It is for the middle-aged manager that career development becomes a crisis and it is to his plight that we shall devote the remainder of this chapter.

As he reaches higher levels of the hierarchy, the middle-aged manager finds that there are fewer promotion opportunities open to him. The jobs that are available are bigger and take longer to master; he may well stay long enough in each to find time to consolidate and further develop it, something he has not been used to doing. Person-related factors can also act to slow his career pace. At work he may find his abilities declining or his technological knowledge becoming outdated; he may not be motivated to learn new skills or accommodate to new management regimes. At home he may have lost his position as sole decision maker, as his family becomes more aware of (and susceptible to) the disruptive effects of moving and resist relocation. The manager typically finds this slowing of his career progress frustrating; for the same inputs of time and energy (which the company still expects) he is receiving fewer rewards of the kind he has learned to accept as payment. The disappointment of the average manager may well be aggravated by the fact that it is at this stage that those with "board potential" start to break away from their contemporaries. The current trend to younger senior managers and board members and the introduction of early retirement schemes have helped to make an increasing number of middle-aged executives feel that they are already obsolete. For many managers this is also a time of evaluation of their success in life as a whole, a time to count their achievements, regret missed opportunities and come to terms with a restricted future (this so-called male menopause is receiving increasing attention in the literature: Constandse, 1972; Wagstaff, 1976; Bowskill and Linacre, 1976). A reappraisal and reordering of priorities is almost inevitable at this stage as the manager enters the final phase of his career, a phase in which company expectations of his behavior, in their turn, will change and require him to make further accommodations. The majority of older employees are not required to show the same dedication to work that they did in their thirties. Unless executives achieve their peak, their career ceiling, as they near retirement, they represent a potential embarrassment to the company. If they stay in their senior positions for too long, they block the promotion prospects of future generations, yet they are not keen to move sideways, even if positions can be

95

found for them, and extremely reluctant to be demoted.

Attitudes and expectations will change with time and in response to changing circumstances, but they will do so too late to help our current generation of middle-aged managers. The latter started their working lives in the belief that they would continue to progress gradually upward until they retired (and some still will do in more traditional companies in which promotion is strictly age related); many are, however, now discovering that the rules have changed, the tables have been turned. Current economic problems, the need to swiftly slim down over-staffed organizations, have served to accelerate to a painful jolt more gradual societal trends. Many companies would like to be able to switch off their older managers and cannot understand why so many of them continue to look to work for their major source of life satisfaction and want a job that they can take home in the evenings and by which they will be pushed to their limits. Having been positively reinforced for such behavior for so long, older managers find it difficult to suddenly alter their life-style. The psychological implications of retirement are now more fully understood (e.g., Havighurst, Munnichs, Neugarten and Thomas, 1969), and more and more companies are taking care to prepare the employee, and sometimes his wife as well, for this significant life change. Expecting a manager to take his job less seriously at the age of 50 or 55 is a similar, but usually less explicit, request for adaptation and one which many fight hard to ignore. Society's norms (that pay increases and promotion are the main rewards for performing well in a job), which managers themselves foster, are perhaps the most to blame for this misunderstanding, but the company must also take re-sponsibility as the immediate reinforcer of these norms.

What does the manager do to cope with this disequi-librium in his relationships with the company? The most successful strategy (in his life as a whole as well as at work) appears to be acceptance of his limitations and a more or less conscious decision to balance decreasing satisfaction from one life area with increasing involvement in an-other. Some look for this within the work context and take greater pride in the nonaspiring facets of their jobs (often relationships with like-situated colleagues and their roles as developers of subordinates); some turn to their families and spend more time with them; some develop their in-terests outside work. Forces and experiences other than career frustration contribute to and help growth in such directions. Conscious of growing older the manager may seek to enjoy to the full the experiences he has and come to place more emphasis on the here-and-now and less on possible future rewards. Training (particularly of the T-group, interpersonal skills type) may prompt an interest in personal growth and other people and a veering away from more materialistic values. As the children grow up and leave home his wife may become a more demanding companion. The manager may feel that too great a dedi-cation to work is depriving him of satisfaction from other life areas and may act to redress this balance.

The alternative to acceptance and constructive cop-ing for the middle-aged manager who is not one of the few who can leave the company and continue (or start again) elsewhere is frustration and rebellion. Trying previously successful policies—working hard, office politics and lobbying those in power—is unlikely to get him noticed in the way he desires. Losing enthusiasm he may psychologically withdraw, risking being judged incompetent at his present level (and the possibility of demotion) if his job performance suffers as a result. The individual experiencing this phase of his career may well feel that he is having to cope with failure; this is only *truly* so if he has been treated unfairly and/or the goals toward which he was working were realistic. This brings us to the problem with which we should like to round off this section—that of individual versus company responsibility. The central theme so far has been the control the company exercises over the manager's working life and the ways in which this might cause him stress. The individual has been mentioned in passing but rather as a predominantly receiving, sometimes reactive, element in the relationship. What of his responsibility to manage his own life, particularly as its course over time (and probably between companies) is concerned? The balancing of freedom with dependency is itself a potential source of stress. The manager who is aware that he is staying in a dissatisfying job, because he lacks the courage to look outside, would receive less pay elsewhere or whatever, adds to the pressures from his job that of knowing that he has the option to leave. A way of avoiding at least this potential stressor is to become wholly dependent on the company, having faith that one will be treated fairly. Employers are often willing to adopt the paternalistic role into which such employee needs casts them; it means that they can operate more secretively and with less deliberation and debate as they do not have to listen to individuals' opinions. It is when something goes wrong and the manager feels that he is not being fairly rewarded that the role becomes difficult. If he is someone who externalizes (rather than internalizes) blame, he is more than likely to direct it at the company. (In contrast, Sofer, 1970, reports that luck is usually seen as responsible for success.) In many respects it would, therefore, be to the company's advantage if its employees would take on more responsibility for their own development. Living in a self-conscious age, we may well find that managers do come to plan their careers (and their lives) more deliberately. By so doing they will cause problems for the companies within which they choose to exercise this freedom, but may relieve the latter of the responsibility for providing the extensive financial and social support systems which are coming to be expected; they may come to believe with Forster (1951) that "Spoonfeeding in the long run teaches us nothing but the shape of the spoon."

5

THE WORK: HOME INTERFACE

Our consideration of stress so far has looked inward at the manager's working life within the organization. Taking a broader view of the individual, we shall now turn to those potential stressors which act at the interface between his two main life areas—work and home. In the first half of the chapter we shall be dealing with the average manager —a man (as yet few women have reached senior levels) married to a woman who is principally home oriented (the full dual-career marriage is, as yet, a deviant pattern), having approximately two children and finding little time for activities outside his work and home lives (Marshall and Cooper, 1976a). Later we shall look more closely at differences within the group.

Managerial jobs are, as we have seen, usually poorly defined in terms of content, time and place. There is always more to be done if the occupant is willing; no external authorities prescribe the maximum number of hours the manager should work and the job is not tied to a particular location; it can be taken home, onto trains and planes, anywhere the manager himself goes. Lacking the specific guidelines of those in other types of work, the manager must decide how much of his life, in terms of both time and energy, his job should take up. In doing so he must balance, though he will seldom do so consciously, a host of considerations. The most obvious are the job demands themselves—the things that have to be done. Secondly, he must take into account his own characteristics: his ability (e.g., if he finds report writing difficult he may need to take it home where he can concentrate more easily); his motivations (conscientious managers are not satisfied unless a piece of work has been done well; the ambitious may perform in the same way but for different reasons, etc.). Thirdly, there are the other demands on his time and energy, principally, in this context, those from his wife and family. This is not a decision that can be made at one point in time and adhered to; it must be remade each time there are fluctuations in any of the salient variables. For the typical manager, achieving an acceptable balance is, then, a continual source of conflict and a potential source of stress. The main theme of this chapter is how the manager manages his allocation of time and energy, balancing the often conflicting demands of work and home about the point of his own motivations, and what implications this has for the two systems in which he is involved.

Focusing on the manager as the occupant of an organizational role, let us look first at the ways in which work intrudes into the home. The most obvious is when the manager takes work home in the evenings and on weekends. Managers often complain that they cannot get

101

work done at work (Marshall, 1977). Looking to Minzberg (1973) for an analysis of how managers actually spend their time, we find that the bulk of the day is taken up with interaction (in large companies scheduled and un-scheduled meetings took up a total of 69 percent of the manager's working day), and that the time spent continuously in any one activity is short (90 percent being devoted to activities lasting less than nine minutes). While such a pattern of time allocation seems to be almost intrinsic to the managerial role, it leaves little opportunity to settle down to two other important facts of the job: (1) the routine paper work and reading (of which as organizations get bigger, and knowledge and consultation proliferate, there seems to be always more) and (2) the special tasks (writing reports, preparing for important meetings) for which concentration is required. Even if he is not overloaded by his job, the manager may prefer to save these tasks until he can do them in peace, quickly and efficiently. This may either be when everyone else has gone home or, if he prefers to keep more normal hours and see his children, later in the evening as an alternative to television. For many managers work is an accepted *and enjoyed* leisure activity. Control is the important factor here. If the manager works at home because he feels he has no choice (to keep up to date, etc.), actually having to do so will probably be a source of stress for him. If he does so truly voluntarily, ill effects, if there are any, will come from other sources—its effects on his health or his relationship with a wife who feels neglected, perhaps. Taking work home, the ever-present briefcase in the living room, can mean that the manager, especially during the week, finds it difficult to "switch off." For those who have this problem, and the implication is that it is a common one, Wright (1975b) suggests the use of alcohol in modest doses.

The wife of the hypothetical manager described above may well feel that he is a cohabitant rather than a companion. If she accepts that the manager's work takes precedence over their joint life, she is likely to develop her own separate activities to keep her busy until he is free to be with her. If, however, she is jealous, she has considerable power to put him under pressure from the home side. Should she choose to do so, the manager may find that because his work: home conflict has been explicitly stated, he must either act to achieve some long-term, rather than the usual *ad hoc,* resolution or must face the consequences of living with an acknowledged disagreement. Even if he does not take work home as an activity, the manager, in his mood and his attitudes, is unlikely to leave it totally behind. The mood of the day, whether it is irritation or satisfaction, depression or elation, will be transported into the home environment and may well affect the lives of those there. Miller (Owen, 1976) goes further to suggest that the nature of the job one does affects one's personality and hence behavior at home. Those in entrepreneurial jobs, he claims, are characterized by responsibility, initiative and flexibility; in contrast "the bureaucratic man is passive and does nothing independently."

A second intrusion of work into home life is business travel. The requirements for this vary considerably between jobs. The salesman, liaising with other companies, is the archetype of the employee whose work and home lives are dominated by travel (Nichols, 1971; Miller, 1949). In large firms consultation between divisions is also common. International travel, too, is becoming increasingly important. For the manager travel has many benefits. While most agree that it is not subsidized sightseeing in the full sense of the term, many are glad of the opportunity to see new places and experience new customs. Living in hotels and eating and drinking on expense accounts also has a certain attraction, as does the freedom from family responsibilities and ties. Most executives agree, however, that the glamor palls after a while, the disadvantages (fatigue, the strains and uncertainties of negotiating with foreigners, returning to a mountain of accumulated work and missing home life, for example) become more powerful disincentives. At home his wife is not only robbed of her husband's company, she is also left to cope with running the home and looking after the family alone. This can cause practical problems, if the house or car needs repair, for example. If she is a little nervous, merely the thought that some emergency may arise while she is on her own, can be a source of stress to her. Young children react badly to disruption; a typical fear is that daddy will not come back, and they may need to be treated especially carefully while he is away from home. This puts the wife under the added burden of needing to be even stronger and more stable than usual.

Even if she has the time to do so, the manager's wife is unlikely to continue an active social life while he is away. Getting a baby-sitter involves so many problems that she is likely to save the precious outing until they can go together. She may also find that there are few places to go—middle-class social life is based on the couple as a unit and cannot easily adapt to involve half-couples as individuals in their own right. If travel is uncertain and planned only at the last moment, its social disruption effects are likely to be even more marked. This is not to say that all wives suffer by being left alone occasionally; some enjoy the opportunities their husbands' absences afford them to be by themselves for a while (Nichols, 1971) and may take pride in the independence they learn with time (Marshall and Cooper, 1976a). Many, however, do not accept and seek to make the most of such situations. Especially if she is unhappy with her role, the manager's wife may be jealous of her husband's freedom and opportunities for adventure (Guest and Williams, 1973). This can put an added strain on their relationship at times of separation. If she makes this resentment explicit, her husband may feel pressured into pretending to her that he, too, dislikes traveling and finds it a chore, in contradiction to the relatively positive attitudes he expresses at work. Such conflicts are among the reasons which prompt managers to segregate their home and work lives and can make their wives feel even more excluded from the real world.

A further intrusion into the manager's home life is the social part of his work role. He may be required to attend social engagements in the evenings—official dinners, entertaining visitors, etc. Sometimes he must go alone which keeps him away from home (robbing the family of yet more time together); at other times his wife may be required to go along and play the manager's wife.

105

Some wives like to become involved in this way and take on the role with pleasure; many, however, resent being treated as if they had no identity of their own and steer as well clear as they can of such obligations. American companies have always placed much emphasis on wives' suitability for such backup duties. Whyte (1951) reports that half the companies he surveyed screened wives as part of their executive hiring procedures. (Even if social engagements take place during the day, they are not without their implications for home life. Although the manager's wife does not stand behind the door with a rolling pin awaiting his drunken return from a business lunch, she may well, however, be upset if he cannot eat the meal to which she has dedicated much of her afternoon.)

The fourth intrusion of significance in the context of this book is the effect decisions made at work have on home life. Accepting promotion, for example, usually means working harder, and consequently neglecting family life, for at least a few months; if it also requires moving to a new area of the country, its repercussions may be extreme. Companies typically negotiate with the manager, in such matters, as if he were a free agent, ignoring the fact that he is part of a larger unit. In bygone days he may well have been the chief decision maker and have, therefore, been empowered to enter into contracts on the family's behalf. Writers suggest that it is the manager's wife who bears the brunt in such situations (Pahl and Pahl, 1971; Seidenberg, 1973) and that he does not always realize what is involved. The manager's power has, however, now been seriously eroded, firstly, by the emancipation of his children, and now by that of his wife. Companies are likely to find their employees increasingly less malleable as more needs, but especially those of the wife's own career, are legitimated and have to be satisfied.

Summarizing the points made so far, we find that the manager's job tends to dominate his life at home as much as in his official work place. It not only takes up a considerable amount of his time and energy, it also dictates how his wife and family will structure their lives. In order to support his chosen life-style and work load, the manager both diverts energy away from his home life and demands extra energy resources of it. At the most basic level he expects a certain standard of home comforts. His job keeps him too busy to take on responsibility for most of these functions himself and so he must rely on his wife to provide them. Gowler and Legge (1975) have referred to the tacit understanding that his wife should act as a support team so that the manager can fill his demanding job as "the hidden contract." In addition to satisfaction of his physical needs, the manager needs a certain measure of social support if he is to cope with work pressure. (Caplan, Cobb and French, 1975 and Wright, 1975b, from widely different data bases, suggest that this is an extremely important variable in the mediation of stress.) If his job is a trying one he may well look to home as a haven of rest and recuperation; it will be important, therefore, that while there he is protected as far as possible from problems and confrontation. It is often a wife's responsibility to act as a buffer between her husband and the children when he first comes home in the evening and just wants to be left alone. She may be expected to hide her own stresses as

107

well so as not to overburden him. In the report, *The Management Threshold,* Beattie et al. (1974) suggest that it is particularly in his early career development that the manager needs such protection, but that this is also a taxing time for his wife as she tries to cope with a young family. They go on to suggest that in order to insulate themselves from each others' pressures at this time of peak demand, the couple adopt a distanced style of relating. Other writers also suggest that detachment can be a way of coping with stress (Handy, 1975; Cooper and Marshall, 1977), but that this will not stand the couple in particularly good stead for tackling interactive problems at later life stages.

We have so far considered the manager as a "carrier" from work to home. Is there evidence of traffic in the reverse direction? It would seem likely that problems at home will affect the manager's work performance, but we know of no research which explicitly investigates this issue. Assuming for the moment, though, that home does intrude into work, we can expect it to do so either actively or passively. For example, active intrusion would be when the manager worries so much about a child's illness that he cannot perform well in his job or when he loses work time as he looks for a new house. Passive intrusion is more subtle; it is when home life fails to defer to work if the latter's precedence has not been established. The manager's is just one of society's roles currently undergoing radical changes. As his behavior becomes more a matter of constant choice and less of established precedent, we can expect it to become more of a problem to him. How he chooses will affect the organization for which he works.

Companies will soon have to decide how they are going to cope with managers who leave being ambitious to their wives, or take time off work to look after ill children because her job is the more lucrative.

Throughout the above discussion in which we have been concentrating on the needs of the manager as an organizational member, we have implied that home, in its turn, is making demands on his time and energy. His wife will have expectations of him as a husband, companion and, probably, a handyman about the house; both she and the children will make demands on him in his role as father. What these demands will be will vary greatly with the life stage the family is at. Guest and Williams (1973) map out the waxing, waning and interacting of work and family demands for the typical manager. Here we should like to incorporate this life-stage approach into a wider framework, taking into account, also, trends in society over time. The model presented is based on the assumption that the role the manager's wife adopts is the crucial factor determining how the couple handles the demands on their joint system; it is expressed, therefore, in terms of the potential roles open to her today. The implications of her choice not only for the wife and husband concerned but also for the organization for which the manager works will be discussed.

In Figure 5.1 managers' wives' potential roles are depicted by boxes and organized along two axes: a time dimension from the past to the future and the family life cycle from early marriage through childbearing and rearing to the empty nest (i.e., couples with children at home but relatively independent and those whose children

109

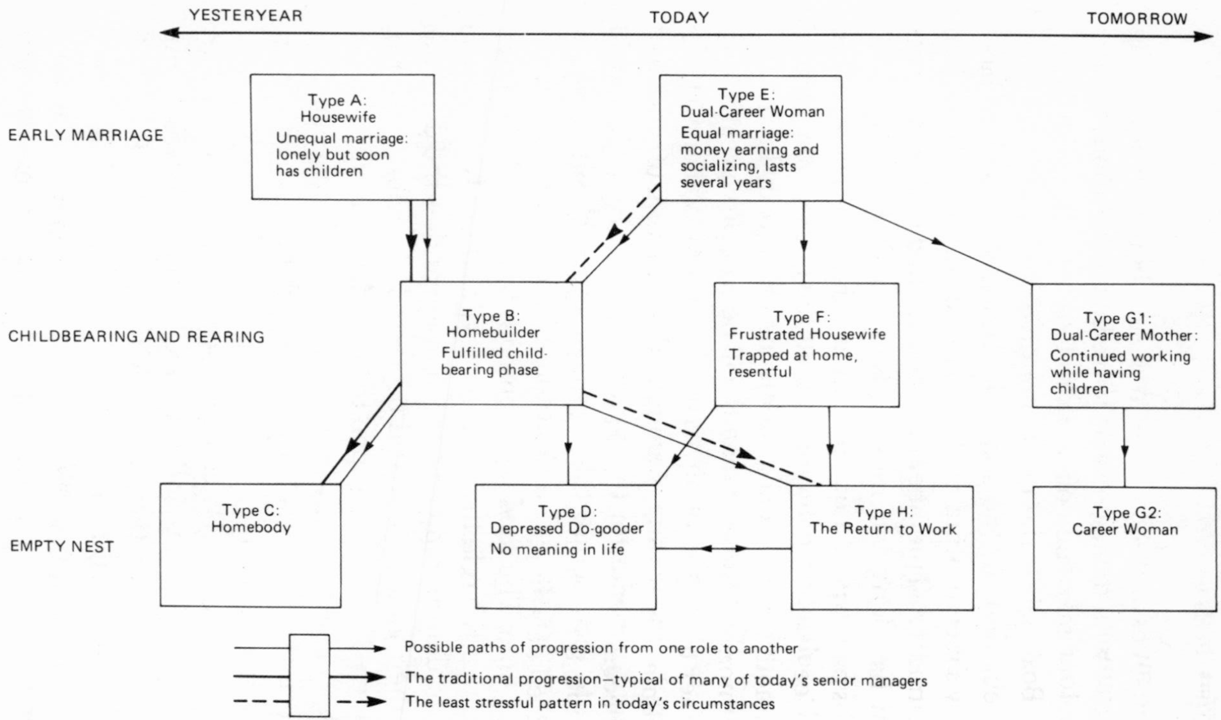

YESTERYEAR | TODAY | TOMORROW

EARLY MARRIAGE

Type A:
Housewife
Unequal marriage: lonely but soon has children

Type E:
Dual-Career Woman
Equal marriage: money earning and socializing, lasts several years

Type G1:
Dual-Career Mother: Continued working while having children

Type G2:
Career Woman

CHILDBEARING AND REARING

Type B:
Homebuilder
Fulfilled child-bearing phase

Type F:
Frustrated Housewife
Trapped at home, resentful

Type D:
Depressed Do-gooder
No meaning in life

Type H:
The Return to Work

EMPTY NEST

Type C:
Homebody

——— Possible paths of progression from one role to another
━━━ The traditional progression—typical of many of today's senior managers
- - - The least stressful pattern in today's circumstances

Figure 5.1 Roles open to the manager's wife

110

have moved away).* The thin lines and arrows in the diagram indicate possible paths of progression from one role to another.

Boxes A, B, C, D and H are sufficient to describe the present and past roles of the vast majority of wives of today's senior managers. The progression from A to B to C is traditional for this middle-class group. The wife typically has a job before she marries, but not one to which she is particularly committed; it is more likely to be of the service type (that of nurse, teacher or secretary) with poor promotional prospects, requiring little involvement outside normal working hours and acting as a suitable forerunner to raising children and managing the problems of a home and husband. On marrying she gives up this job to become a full-time housewife, her "true" vocation. This is not, usually, as exciting and fulfilling as she had expected and may be a particularly lonely time for her (especially if promotions move the couple away from her supportive family and friends and into hostile, nonmobile areas of the country). While the housewife may envy her husband his job and freedom, she fundamentally accepts her role as a supportive wife and housekeeper and, by performing well in it, frees her husband to devote himself fully to developing his career. She, meantime, participates in his success both for the improvement it brings in their standard of living and the status it confers. Above all, though, the housewife looks forward to starting a family. Being a homebuilder is, then, a demanding but fulfilling

*Part of this material was drawn from an article published by the authors in *Management International Review,* vol. 1, 1977.

time for her. The young wife's preoccupation now paral- lels her husband's involvement in his work and the couple are likely to cope with their work loads and stresses sepa- rately. The role segregation in which this results probably means that, psychologically, they seldom meet; their rela- tionships are complementary rather than shared. If the wife is willing to continue to maintain a supportive role vis-a-vis her husband as the children become indepen- dent and move away from home, she can be described as a contented homebody. She may take on outside activities to help fill her day as her family duties decrease but her main concern will be that these should not interfere with the (limited) time she spends with her husband. In this type of marriage the couple continue in their comple- mentary roles; his career success satisfies them both (she may well take on a social role in relation to his job) and the organization benefits by getting one and a half em- ployees for the price of one.

Types D and H deviate somewhat from this tradi- tional pattern. There is little to distinguish the depressed do-gooder from the contented homebody in the way she spends her day; the fundamental difference is, though, that the former does not find the things she does fulfilling. While the latter has built up a meaningful identity, the former has somehow failed to do so. At this stage many wives take on a job, usually part time, to fill the gap in their lives (the return to work) and, although they may have initial problems in balancing home and work de- mands, find that both they and their husbands benefit from their decision to do so. For those who cannot take such a step, this can be an exceptionally unhappy and depressing time. Their husbands may not be sympathetic to these rather vague identity problems or may be going through similar problems of their own, and the couple's segregated past has given them little practice in dealing with such interpersonal problems.

The common factor in these five boxes is the agreement by manager, wife and his employing company that his job dominates the couple's lives. It is this basic tenet that younger generations are questioning and their difference of opinion is reflected in the new, alternative roles they have opened up. Today's junior manager is likely to marry a dual-career wife. More widely available higher education, the need for two incomes to accumulate capital and their failure to find being just a housewife a meaningful identity prompt most women to continue working after marriage. The wife's attitude at this stage is a key to the couple's future. For some women, a job soon takes second place to husband and home and they opt happily for and derive pleasure from the homebuilder role when it arrives, usually planning to return to work when their children reach high school age. At the other extreme is the dual-career orientation. The wife is heavily involved in her job, devoting substantial amounts of time and energy to it rather than to her home life. The working woman is in a position of obvious role conflict, and the relationship she achieves with her husband will depend largely on his expectations of her as a wife (and mother of his children).

Women's Liberation has thrown men's as much as women's roles into confusion and the position of the former in modern society is by no means free of conflict.

113

While he may subscribe to the "new man" ethic—being happy for his wife to pursue her own career, sharing in the home—maintaining activities and accepting the sacrifices in home comforts this may well necessitate, the career-oriented woman's husband may not be completely independent of society's old norms. We feel that many "new men" show an underlying ambivalence. Few are truly happy to earn less than their wives, most positively reinforce good cooking and housekeeping while denying the importance of such things, and most are happy to be fussed over (in moderation) while still openly affirming the "equalitarian living mate" ideal. The double messages they send, therefore, may well throw their wives into even more confusion (Laing, Ronald and Esterton, 1964).

A critical decision for today's young couple is whether or not to have children. It is those women who decide to do so and then find themselves trapped by their decision who are the casualties of the new mores and are labeled frustrated housewives here. These women not only do not enjoy the day-to-day activities of running a home and raising a family but feel that they are actually suffering from the experience. At the same time a conscientious approach to motherhood prevents them from escaping. A wife in this situation may well jealously vent some of her wrath on her husband by actively withholding her support; rather than helping him cope with work stress, she adds to his problems. The strain this situation puts on the couple's relationship will probably only be removed by time, when the wife eventually comes to feel that she will not be neglecting her children by returning to work.

114

The alternative open to her, to follow a continuous dual-career progression with short interruptions for child-bearing, involves several problems in addition to those already mentioned for the childless dual-career marriage. First, child rearing (unlike dish washing) cannot be neglected without risking serious repercussions. To date there have been no large-scale developments of adequate surrogate care facilities. Second, the woman's decision to continue, rather than break and resume, her work means that she is as able to successively develop a career as is her husband; this intensifies the problems of her time/involvement management and his susceptibility to feel threatened by her competition. Third, compared to the household of the frustrated housewife where the norm is that the manager's job should be denied importance and underperformance is therefore encouraged, the husband of a career woman is likely to be expected to place a high emphasis on his work, devote time to it and succeed. In this situation the manager could well push himself more at work, courting the strain of overpromotion. Unlike the husband of the homebuilder, he will lack the backup of a supportive wife with plenty of time to help him cope with work stresses (she may well have plenty of her own) and a ready-made social world in which he can unwind. It may also become important not to be left behind if his wife is successful. Fourth, sheer capacity problems may well mean that the couple adopt a slightly distanced relationship similar to that seen in Type B (Homebuilder) but without the tacitly agreed priorities of this latter type—decision making in the dual-career family could, therefore, be a traumatically devisive activity. Personality char-

115

acteristics will play a large part in the success or otherwise of this type of marriage. The benefits of a family pattern which simultaneously satisfies the needs of all its members are obvious; if, however, the couple are both achievement oriented and conscientious, they may well take on more than they can jointly manage.

The difference between the left and right hand columns of Figure 5.1 is, then, a generation gap. In today's circumstances the least stressful pattern would appear to be E to B to H/G2, shown here by a dotted line. Whatever role his wife adopts, however, we see that today's manager is likely to have less time and energy to devote to work, and to receive less support from home in the performance of his job. In contrast, what most organizations demand and expect of their managers in return for success and promotion has not changed dramatically over the last thirty years. (It must be noted that here we assume that most managers view their jobs as major sources of life satisfaction and are sufficiently ambitious to follow a developing, expanding and fulfilling career throughout their working lives—we are, therefore, concentrating on the man who wants to move up.) Organizations expect their managers to become highly involved in the success of the company and of their job in particular. They are expected to display their involvement and dedication by heavy investments of emotional energy and time, working in the evenings and on weekends when necessary, traveling on company business, spending appropriate time on work-related social activities (usually unaccompanied) and responding enthusiastically to company offers of promotion or geographic mobility. Any time they do have free should be spent in rest and recuperation to enable them to come back refreshed and ready for further company service. In view of this, let us look again at the various possibilities offered in Figure 5.1 and summarize their likely consequences for the manager, his wife and the organization for which the former works. Figure 5.2 presents our suggestions as to who wins, winning essentially meaning the matching of expectations and needs, whatever these may be, with reality.

We see that, while the traditional marriage progression $(A \rightarrow B \rightarrow C)$ might lack some of the personal contact and growth elements advocated today, it was, overall, beneficial to both partners and to the company. In it roles were complementary, relationships were fundamentally in balance and the manager was released by his hidden contract to dedicate most of his time to following organizational goals. The wife who does not accept the homebody role may, unhappily, become a depressed dogooder, but this occurs too late to have any dramatic effects on the manager and his work, although it might reduce the level of social support he receives at home. Her solution, to return to work, may, in fact, be more disruptive as it threatens not only his social but his physical home comforts. The outcome of such a development will depend on the new balance of priorities the couple achieve. It is unlikely, after so long, that his job will be ousted from dominance and the manager may well reap considerable benefits from having a more satisfied wife.

In the boxes representing today, the outcomes, especially those for the manager and his organization, are much less certain. Looking at the wife's roles, the assump-

117

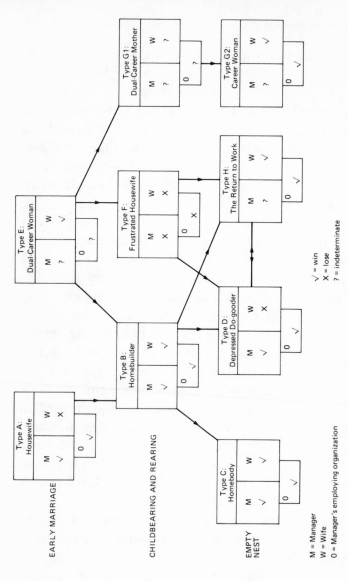

Figure 5.2 "Who-Wins Table": Managers' wives' roles and win/lose consequences for the manager, wife, and organization

M = Manager
W = Wife
O = Manager's employing organization

√ = win
X = lose
? = indeterminate

EARLY MARRIAGE

Type A:
Housewife

M	W
√	X
O	√

Type E:
Dual-Career Woman

M	W
?	√
O	?

Type G1:
Dual-Career Mother

M	W
?	?
O	?

Type G2:
Career Woman

M	W
?	√
O	√

CHILDBEARING AND REARING

Type B:
Homebuilder

M	W
√	√
O	√

Type F:
Frustrated Housewife

M	W
X	X
O	X

Type D:
Depressed Do-gooder

M	W
√	X
O	√

Type H:
The Return to Work

M	W
?	√
O	√

EMPTY NEST

Type C:
Homebody

M	W
√	√
O	√

118

tion is that she is career oriented; it is, therefore, only in the frustrated housewife box that she definitely loses. Being a dual-career mother is likely to be a strain (Rapoport and Rapoport, 1976) but highly rewarding. The outcome for the manager depends on his ordering of priorities between work and home (we tend to believe that he too may feel confused about what this is). If he is work oriented he is likely to lose as the shared family pattern (though bringing satisfactions of its own) reduces the amount of time and energy he can devote to his job. If his wife is dissatisfied with her role, he may even find that she is actively discouraging him from performing well. If he too values the new, home-oriented life-style he may win, but at the expense of being as successful in his career as he could have been. The organization's goals are assumed to have changed very little over the last thirty years; we see that, in the short-term at least, it stands to lose from any role combination which threatens to reduce the manager's involvement in work. It may in the long-term, however, reap the benefits of more harmonious family relationships. As Gavron (1966) suggests in her book on *The Captive Wife,* the social change which is encouraging women to play a more active role in industrial life creates problems, particularly "by advancing more quickly on some fronts than others." Managers and their wives are currently facing a major redefinition of their roles; the organizations for which they will *both* soon work have yet to appreciate that they too will feel the effects of the problems this is bringing.

6

STRESSFUL EVENTS: A CASE STUDY OF THE MOBILE MANAGER AND HIS WIFE

> Temporal factors are crucial, and manifold, in research on human stress. . . . Yet, very little consideration has been given to such temporal factors in theory or in research. . . . Time may be one of the most important and most neglected parameters of the problem. (McGrath, 1970c)

Life is a continuing dynamic interaction of organism with environment rather than a sequence of disconnected stable states. So far, we have largely failed to reflect this by taking a snapshot approach to the understanding of stress. Here we should like to attempt to redress this balance by considering, briefly, some of the facets of time as an important interacting variable and then going on to describe in more detail the development of a potentially stressful event, the relocation of a manager and his family.

TIMING FACTORS

Timing is, firstly, important because it determines into which of the organism's ongoing activities the potential stressor intrudes. Just as our metabolisms are more capable of withstanding the shock of treatment at certain phases of the circadian rhythm than at others (Luce, 1973), so our current psychological and social state can make us more or less vulnerable to pressure. The manager who is facing problems at home is an obvious example: an additional, but at other times innocuous, demand such as a business trip abroad may put him in an intolerable situation. Similarly, the decision whether or not to accept an offered relocation and promotion will be a difficult one for the employee who has not fully mastered the position he has. Only the focal individual can judge the full impact of each additional demand made on his system, and even his perception may be unrealistically distorted by optimism, pessimism or whatever. The dividing line between challenge and stress is a delicate one, and at work much relies on the manager's immediate superior's ability to be aware of his subordinate's capabilities, *au fait* with his current circumstances, and sensitive to the initial signs of strain so that he can time his demands knowingly if not conveniently.

A second time-related variable is whether a pressure is acute, recurrent or chronic and which of these three categories the resulting stress, if any, can be classed under. Relocation is an acute pressure, taking place within a relatively brief time period. Its immediate discomforting effects—separation, house hunting, etc.—are

121

made more tolerable because they are known to be temporary. When a new state of balance is achieved, the acute pressure is usually forgotten; if, however, something goes wrong—the new house is unsuitable in some respect or the event causes an irreparable rift in the couple's relationship—it can have serious, long-term ill effects. Acute pressures are, then, the more easily manageable of the three types. Some jobs are characterized by recurrent pressures, the accountant with month- and year-end deadlines, for example. Expecting and being able to plan for such pressures removes much of their sting. A recurrent pressure which typically arrives intermittently and unexpectedly is, in contrast, more difficult to cope with. Industrial relations problems fit into this category; in some industries they are an ever-present threat to management. A poor relationship with a colleague can have a similar effect; it may be adequate to sustain normal day-to-day exchanges, but become critical when one has to work closely with him or finds oneself competing with him for a decision or promotion. A pressure which is present all the time can be termed chronic; if it is judged stressful by the individual it will, by definition, lead to chronic stress. The physical danger in mining is of this type; if the pressure is unavoidable, as this largely is, the most adaptive strategy for the employee is to accommodate to it, reappraising it psychologically as nonstressful. Managers adapting to chronic pressures—responsibility, making decisions, having to devote a lot of time to work —in this way will typically say that "this is what I'm paid for," "its part of the job." In his experiments with "executive" monkeys, Brady (1966) found that intermittent pressure was more likely to create ulcers than was chronic pressure and suggested that in the latter situation, despite unpleasant circumstances, some type of stable adjustment occurred. It is sometimes difficult, without outside help, to differentiate the inevitable from the unnecessary chronic pressures. When researchers talk about improving the quality of working life (O'Toole, 1974), it is usually toward the latter that they direct their immediate attention.

A third timing factor is whether the elements in a potentially stressful pattern of pressures act sequentially or simultaneously. The individual is more likely to be overwhelmed if several pressures act at once than if his "assumptive world" or Life Space (Parkes, 1971) is only affected a piece at a time. He may, however, stand a better chance of regrouping optimally if all areas of his life are in a state of flux at the same time (De Bono, 1970). From their research into life changes and the subsequent development of illness, a group of workers at Washington University (for a review see Holmes and Masuda, 1973) suggest that it is the amount of change per se that has harmful effects. Their work did not, however, fully investigate the intricacies of the issue, and other writers would contend that repeated minor calls on the organism to adapt will be more wearing and result in a less good final state than one massive demand for reorganization (Rapoport and Rapoport, 1964). Motivation for change will be an important intervening variable affecting ultimate success. Viewed in these terms the manager and his wife's experiences of relocation are qualitatively different. He is committed to the change which affects only part of his life. She, in contrast, faces a complete disruption of her

123

previous identity and is likely to have few firsthand reasons for wanting to do so.

A final consideration to which we should like to draw the reader's attention is the timing of the stressed individual's coping response. (Lipawski, 1969, reminds us that the organism's reaction is an integral part of the situation: How a person experiences the pathological process, what it means to him, and how this meaning influences his behavior and interaction with others are all integral components of disease viewed as a total human response.) Coping does not just happen after the event; it can also take place before and during the stress experience, can be anticipatory or preventative, can be directed either at the environment or at the consequences, one or several coping techniques can be adopted and multiple techniques can be simultaneous or successive. Anticipatory coping is particularly appropriate to relocation as a potentially stressful event. Hamburg and Adams (1967) describe some of the role and information manipulation strategies used by students in the summer vacation between high school and college to prepare for their new lives. In similar ways the manager and his family, once they know they are leaving, shut down their relationship with the old job, house, social life, etc., and start acquiring information about the new location. Anticipatory coping would, at first glance, seem to be a particularly good idea. It does, however, have certain drawbacks:

1. The individual may not perform as well in the present if he is focusing his efforts on the future.

2. He may be mistaken in his expectations and his plans may be useless or grossly inappropriate.
3. He may miss the potential for change and growth in a situation by treating it with old, well-established rules.

RELOCATION

The potentially stressful event we have chosen as an illustration is relocation, a move between two geographically separated sites, branches or whatever of the same company. Mobility is an inescapable fact of managerial life. Pahl and Pahl (1971) report that 22 percent of their sample of middle-class managers had moved workplace every two or three years and a further 33 percent once every four or five years. Birch and Macmillan (1970) in a survey of 2,000 managers found wide variations but overall a high incidence of movement—on the average, their sample had changed employers 2.7 times per career and jobs within a company 2.9 times per career. Sixty-six percent of the managers contacted by Seidenberg (1973) expected to move every three years. As moving is an event which takes place over a protracted but definable time period, it is relatively accessible to study. It is also a particularly apposite subject here as the whole family is involved, and this gives us the opportunity to build on the themes of the preceding chapter by treating the manager as part of this wider social unit. Rather than look in detail

125

at the scanty, but multidisciplinary, literature on this topic, which we have done elsewhere (Marshall and Cooper, 1976b), we prefer here to adopt a case study approach, drawing on results from a qualitative research study of managers moving between the various sites of a large company (Marshall and Cooper, 1976a*). We shall, then, follow the average manager, his wife and two children through a hypothetical move. In line with the emphasis of this book we shall concentrate more on the negative aspects, the problems involved, but we shall also seek to do justice, if in less detail, to the many short- and long-term pleasant facets and benefits of moving.

Events and their effects will be discussed in three temporal phases according to whether they occur before, during or after the move. Within each of these sections we shall consider the activities and tasks to be accomplished, their meaning for the manager, his wife and children, and the outcomes for the various family members. Figure 6.1 locates the potential causes of stress during relocation and factors which help to mitigate its effects for the two main people, the manager and his wife, in this underlying structure.

Before the Move

It is the manager's decision to take up a new position which sets the process of moving in motion and for him the single most important factor, throughout, is his job. In most organizations moving is an essential ingredient of

*Part of the material that follows was published by the authors as an MCB Monograph and first appeared as *Management Decision,* vol. 14, no. 4, 1976.

career development and the employee learns to accept this if he wants to move up. Most managers' careers can be seen schematically as a recurring cycle:

feel ready for a new job
↓
accept new job ⟶ face challenge ⟶ succeed ⟶ run job smoothly
↓
need fresh job opportunities

Few managers appear to be happy filling a job which does not stretch them fully. After an appropriate time in one position (the two to three years necessary to master it), they are carefully assessing their situation and what the future holds. If their present company cannot offer them advancement, they may well be swift to look outside for opportunities. If the manager with "itchy feet" is offered within the company a promotion which requires moving to a new site, he is, then, unlikely to refuse. He may have certain regrets—e.g., leaving a harmonious work team or a project unfinished—but he is soon likely to become future oriented. If an offered position is not obviously an advancement, he may be more reluctant to accept. He may, for example, doubt whether there is a real job for him to go to, see the new post as a demotion or be confused about its benefits because it would disqualify him from consideration for an impending vacancy he has set his sights on. His decision may be made more difficult, too, if his fears are in the opposite direction: if he doubts his capacity to do the offered job (perhaps he feels

127

Figure 6.1

FACTORS WHICH ACCENTUATE OR ATTENUATE THE STRESS INVOLVED IN MOVING
FOR THE MANAGER AND HIS WIFE

THE MANAGER

MINUS	MINUS	MINUS
Happy in previous job	Extra physical demands of travel and extra work	New job makes excessive demands
Reservations about new job (e.g., lateral transfer, no salary increase)	House hunting is difficult and uncertain	Interpersonal problems at work
Doubts ability to master new job	Has to travel on business at time of move	Lacks skills new job requires
Wife reluctant to move (e.g., leaving friends or her job)	Separation	Needs to prove himself quickly
Children at important stage of education	Wife and children unhappy at his absence	Worried that unable to afford new mortgage
Family regard present area as home	Wife jealous of his freedom from responsibility	Concerned because wife and children having problems adapting
Worried about effects on wife and children	Finds it difficult to balance competing demands on his time and interest	Area doesn't offer desired facilities (e.g., sports)

PLUS	PLUS	PLUS
Happy about new job (it was for promotion, etc.)	Enjoys freedom and "bachelor" social life	Job goes well and is satisfying
Loss of motivation for previous job	Involved in new job	New work team provide support
Wife eager to move	House transactions accomplished relatively easily and quickly	Family adapt relatively easily
The move brings benefits to the family (a new house, better schooling)	Makes money on the exchange	

BEFORE THE MOVE	DURING THE MOVE	AFTER THE MOVE
MINUS	MINUS	MINUS
Dislikes upheaval and change	Has to cope with a lot of extra work	Feels lonely and isolated (misses old friends and doesn't make new ones)
Involved in local community	Misses husband	Locals are hostile to strangers
Likes current house	Finds she has little social support in the area	New house unsatisfactory or needs tiring alterations
Works outside the home	Feels that husband does not appreciate her problems, is jealous of his freedom	Dislikes characteristics of the area
Children at critical stage of education	Children upset and miss their father	Husband too involved in new job to give support
Children reluctant to move or react badly to change (she worries about their ability to cope)	House hunting and timing of move are uncertain and exhausting	No job opportunities for her
Lives near her parents		Lives further away from parents
		Children have problems at school (slow to make new friends)
		Husband unhappy in new job
PLUS	PLUS	PLUS
Dislikes current situation (geographic area, house, etc.)	Friends rally round	Befriended by neighbor or company wife
Enjoys change and seeing new places	Separation kept to a minimum by easy transactions, etc.	Already has friends in the area
Likes proposed new location (has friends there)	Finds she can cope and takes pride in her new independence	Makes friends via established channels (the church, baby-sitting club, etc.)
Children will benefit (better quality schooling, can start again if problems at school or with social lives)		Husband and children adapt easily and quickly
		Moves nearer to parents

THE MANAGER'S WIFE

he has not yet mastered the one he has) and realizes that he is risking being overpromoted. The monetary incentive offered to move is an important factor in the decision and reflects these wider considerations. Losing (because of the loss of something such as a company car) or failing to gain money (because the salary increase is minimal) is very poorly regarded. While such circumstances render decision making a more difficult process, it is still unlikely that the manager will eventually refuse to move.* There is a widespread feeling that refusal will adversely affect one's future career prospects, and few people are prepared to take this risk. In addition, managers are in a dependent role in this context and many prefer that the company take on the ultimate responsibility. They assume that higher management has suggested a particular move as part of a longer-term (but essentially well meaning) plan for their development to which they are not party; they may well be flattered by the display of confidence the job offer represents.

The manager may involve his wife in his decision but, typically, she is as dependent on him as he is on the company: neither has a truly effective power of veto. Her initial attitude will depend partly on her personality and partly (and in interaction) on a wide range of situational factors. She may be the kind of person who dislikes instability and change per se; if so she will certainly not welcome the upheaval moving brings. Some women always resist and resent a planned move and suffer badly in the

*Or it was, it appears, that there is a growing, but as yet unexplored, reluctance on the part of today's younger managers to move around the country as requested.

first year in any new location. Usually, though, they then settle down so well that they are equally upset at leaving again. At the other extreme are those wives who welcome change irrespective of its actual content; they are as keen as their husbands to leave after two to three years in one place. Usually the wife's predisposition to move is somewhere between these two extremes and situational factors are more determinant than underlying personality. A felt need for stability or mobility may, for example, be purely a matter of timing. Having to make several moves in rapid succession, particularly for older women who have been through the process many times before, appears to be particularly unsettling, leaving the wife with a need to stay in one place for a substantial period to recuperate. A need for continuity is also seen during critical life phases —pregnancy or a child's first year at school, for example. In the same way, change via mobility is often welcomed for the escape it offers from a current dissatisfaction—an outgrown house, a child who is getting on badly at school, an area of the country one dislikes.

How will circumstances in other life areas act to make the manager's wife more or less willing to move? As for her husband, his job will be a particularly salient dimension. If she is eager for him to get on in the company, the mere fact that the move is for promotion may well be sufficient justification that it is a good thing. Her husband's happiness at work is the major consideration for many wives and knowing that it was what he wanted is adequate reason. If the manager is uncertain about this or is taking on a job which will intrude more into home life than his present one does (in terms of business travel or level of responsibility, for example), his wife is less likely to be convinced that the move will be to their joint benefit.

The wife more than her husband becomes involved in the local community (Packard, 1975); she may do voluntary or even paid work outside the home, and may be reluctant to leave the friends and activities in which she has become involved. It is from such contacts that she derives her separate identity and she may be loath to give this up and have to start again in a new location (Seidenberg, 1972). Family ties play a direct part only in the first move away from home, which female interviewees reported as being a particularly traumatic experience. After this, though, planned moves can affect the extended family network if they move one further away from or nearer to one's parents. "Deserting" them can be a source of guilt, especially as they grow older and more infirm, if there are no brothers or sisters left at home to look after them or they are "robbed" of their grandchildren. A job change that moves the family back to areas which are nearer to relatives, or in which they already have a circle of friends, is likely to be particularly warmly welcomed.

As far as children are concerned, three factors appear to be particularly important in the context of moving: the immediate emotional effects of the experience, education and friendships. In general, children prefer stability to change and uncertainty. Parents usually worried a great deal in advance about how they would cope with the upheaval of the moving period itself and, later, with establishing a life in the new community. The sample as a group placed a high emphasis on education, and for families with certain age groups of children this was a more important factor than house buying in determining when the move actually took place. The start of a new level and the completion of education were the most critical phases and subjects reported deferring moving the family (in a few cases for up to a year) or moving it in advance of the manager to accommodate them. (Moves at crucial change points were welcomed as they made future, harmful changes less likely). The quality as well as the continuity of education is important. It was widely agreed that standards of education vary across regions of the country. A move from a poor to a good area was particularly welcomed, whereas one in the reverse direction was often seen as a problem which required special arrangements. (Managers often feel the need to resort to private education to secure the desired quality and continuity of schooling for their children.) Closely related to education are recreational facilities; these vary not only in quality but also in type with area of the country. Taking children away from their friends was also a worry and this too seemed to be more difficult at certain times than at others. Young children (about three or four years old) who have just made their first friends and teenagers to whom the peer group is particularly important are the most reluctant to leave.

The final major consideration, but one of particular significance to the manager's wife, is the house the family leaves behind. Quitting a house one likes, in which one has invested time and money, can be especially distressing. (Sociologists have gone so far as to compare the grief at loss of a house to bereavement, Fried, 1965.) It is the little things that become important—leaving behind the flowers which have just been planted or the piano, moving the specially tailored piece of furniture that will never fit in properly again. As compensation, a move does give a subsidized opportunity to start again. Many younger couples counted as a major advantage of regular relocation that they were able to get a better house each time.

Balancing out these factors, the manager's wife will be more or less reluctant to move. Her attitude, once formed, will be the chief influence, outside his work, on the manager himself. At a personal level he will, presumably, prefer that she is happy with the plan; at a practical level, he needs at least her cooperation if the move is to be accomplished successfully. Though her power at the decision-making stage may be minimal, later she overpowers her husband in her ability to influence outcomes. The wife is the only family member with both the spare capacity and the experience to organize and handle the mechanics of moving. She is, too, the reservoir of social support for her husband and children and her mood is likely to affect that of the family as a whole. How she approaches the necessary tasks will, then, be an important determinant of how well the family copes with the experience. Typically, the manager's wife accepts a supportive role in relation to her husband's work (Pahl and Pahl, 1971; Marshall, 1977) and, even if unwilling to move, will play down her own needs and concentrate on helping the rest of the family. If, instead, she decides to be uncooperative, this can be a source of considerable stress for her husband and children and make the move more painful than necessary for all concerned.

134

The manager will also have concerns about his children, but he is likely, because of the many other demands on his time, to let his wife mediate between him and them rather than take a direct interest. His relationship with the local community is also rather tenuous. His social life outside work is usually based largely on his wife's contacts, and the sample emphasized that the vast majority of these were acquaintances, not friends. If he does belong to any local associations or clubs, these are likely to be easily transferable—golf, for example. The men's main complaints in this respect were, in fact, about leaving behind good sports facilities or the disruption caused to their competitive year.

The only real activity described for this premoving phase has been that of making the commitment, as a family, to move. A start is usually made to accomplishing the practical tasks—selling and buying a house and arranging schooling for the children—but, in the experience of the sample, these were very seldom completed before the manager moved to his new job, the event we have taken as marking the beginning of the second phase. It is appropriate to note here that the managers from whom this data was collected, typically, moved to their new jobs three to four months before their family was able to join them. It is this period of separation which constitutes the second phase, the move.

The Move

Compared to phase one, during which the load was mainly emotional, this is a period of intense activity. For

135

the manager, his new job is a focal concern. Interviewees reported that they approached new jobs with a mixture of exhilaration and trepidation. It was agreed that the first six months in a new position are particularly crucial. Many mentioned an initial pressure to make one's mark and apprehension because of this. Several younger managers also said that as a "new boy" it was important not to make enemies. The manager must be prepared, for a time, to put in excessive effort for little apparent reward. Certain circumstances served to accentuate this initial trauma. Interviewees reported misgivings about moving if they were not convinced there was a *real* job for them to go to or if they saw the new position as a demotion. Starting a new position can be a particularly stressful time; even if the incumbent is clear about his role, area of action and level of authority, others might not be and this can make it more difficult for him to become established and accepted. (Poorly defined jobs seem to present the same problem for each new manager who fills them.) Changes in function also represent a challenge; for example, if the employee has to learn new skills (which his subordinates have already mastered) or must adopt a new style of working, e.g., work planning after the constant demand situation of implementing, or becoming a manager instead of a doer (several senior accountants said that occasionally they thought how pleasant it would be just to deal with figures again).

Some managers reported special circumstances surrounding a move which caused them problems: moving to a bad atmosphere (especially when this has been created by significant individuals who feel that the new manager is the wrong man for the job); going to work on a product for which there was low demand and, consequently, low morale; going to a position which was a focus of pressure at the time and having no predecessor handy to make learning the new job easier. Moving to a higher management position was not always easy; in several cases this was reported as necessitating a considerable loss of real authority (especially in moves from the factories to the home office) and the more select, but lonelier, life of senior levels was mentioned as an added stress. Certain factors can help to relieve this initial pressure. Knowing the job or aspects of it in advance speeds the learning process. The new work team, or particular members of it, may make an effort to be supportive. If he knows and is already known by his new work colleagues, the manager may feel less pressured to prove himself quickly. Being satisfied that the new position is a promotion, that one is following a traditional career path or that one has the confidence of higher management can also reassure the manager during these early difficult months. Even so, it is typical for a manager to devote even more time and energy than usual to his job in these first six months. His attention is particularly focused on making contacts, becoming known by relevant individuals in the company and learning the new skills required in his position. Many wives mentioned how withdrawn and tired their husbands became at this time and expressed a desire to cushion them from any additional pressures. This was not, however, always possible and managers reported stress from trying to deal with problems both at home and at work.

At the same time that his job is so demanding, the manager has additional out-of-work responsibilities to attend to. As the family's fifth column in the new location, it is usually his responsibility to find a suitable house in a suitable neighborhood. House hunting is a strain on both partners. The couple usually starts out with fairly high ideals, either mimicking an already successful formula or avoiding past mistakes. The critical dimensions of choice appear to be price, physical characteristics (size, etc.), location (nearness to work, good schools, bus services, stores) and type of neighborhood (old town, new housing development). A variety of factors may conspire to make looking for the ideal combination "soul destroying": it may not exist (at least not in that particular part of the country); the house market may be difficult at the time; the couple may lack vital bits of information about the area or the wife may be tied to the (old) house with young children and unable to participate. Above all, though, it is the process of search per se that is time consuming and exhausting. Once a suitable house has been found, the couple face further uncertainties: the disappointment of a contract falling through or the worry that one might do so are major additional strains in an already tense situation. Some couples appear to be prepared to go to any lengths (renting temporary accommodation or having a place built, for example) to get the house they really want. Others adopt a more pragmatic approach and tend to look for an acceptable house to reduce the time of separation, usually aware that it, too, is only a temporary home.

Typically, during the move the manager lives in a hotel in the new location from Monday to Thursday night (traveling home on weekends). Many initially enjoy the relative freedom this means and are glad to take advantage of the increased social and sports opportunities. After a time, however, this "vacation" becomes less pleasant: living continually in a hotel becomes a strain, the manager comes to miss his wife and children (particularly the incentive to relax in the evenings they provide) and traveling home every weekend becomes tiring. In addition, the manager may find that he is under increasing second-hand pressure due to the effects his absence is having on his wife and children.

Most women suffer rather than enjoy this period of separation. The manager's wife finds that she has a lot to do, not only having to cope with the everyday chores (including the "male" half) but also to make preparations for the move. The three major practical worries at this stage are arranging the sale of the current house, participating, at a distance, in buying a replacement, and organizing new schools for the children. Taken together, these determine the timing of the move. Concern for other members of the family may lead her to try and be a more stable influence than usual (especially taking on the additional role of father) and to worry about her husband's traveling. The manager's wife does this at a time when she herself is particularly lonely and deprived of support: she has no adult company in the evenings, no one to turn to in emergencies and no or few opportunities to maintain a satisfying social life. The average case is, we can see, exacting enough but often there are special circumstances which compound the difficulties—being alone with one's first baby or living in an isolated country

139

area, for example. The disruption of home life characteristic of this period also has effects on the children. Young ones may pine for their father, crying when he leaves but failing to recognize him or go to him for attention when he returns. Older children usually hide their fears more cleverly, only to show them by becoming more withdrawn, demanding or aggressive. To an already pressured mother, any such symptoms are an added burden. The wife's practical difficulties are often aggravated by two further problems: (1) uncertainty, particularly as to the timing of the move and (2) her own attitudes, reservations about moving and the nagging suspicion that her husband is enjoying a new freedom which she cannot share. For many couples this complex of pressures makes the precious weekends together highly disturbing and unsatisfactory affairs. Trying to establish contact when one or both partners is feeling tired and/or misunderstood is a challenge to even the best relationships.

For most couples the first few months of separation are the worst. After this, events usually develop to make the situation more acceptable:

1. A routine becomes established.
2. Children settle down and discover that their father does come back after each desertion.
3. The novelty of the husband's freedom wears off slightly and he comes to miss, and express more concern about regaining, his home comforts.
4. House transactions become more definite and encouraging.
5. The wife discovers that she can cope and takes a

pride in her newfound independence and decision-making capacity.

Separation represents a real crisis point in most marriages, however many times it has been experienced in
the past. It is a period of redefining roles and confirming
(or denying) emotional commitment. In many relationships this stressful interlude can have substantial growth
effects; in others, however, it can serve to generate a
distance and conflict which the couple take some time to
resolve

After the Move

Our description of the moving phase has been that
of a host of problems and possible complications and it
is usually a relief for all concerned when the manager
is permanently reunited with his wife and children.
This marks the beginning of the third phase, during
which the family settle in to their new location. For
the manager this usually represents a reduction of direct pressure as he is relieved of the tasks of house
hunting and commuting. He is likely to have more
time to devote to his new job and will now focus in
this direction. His earlier efforts may already be bearing fruit and this will probably be his most stable and
rewarding life area for a while. For his wife the problems change rather than disappear; we shall, then, concentrate on her side of the story and suggest later how
her experiences can feed back to affect the manager.
Adopting a "task accomplishment" approach (Rapoport

141

and Rapoport, 1964), we shall look in turn at the different things she has to achieve in these first few months.

A major part of the manager's wife's day will be spent on establishing the new home. Even if she is home oriented, she may find the unavoidable chores and the expense involved tiresome; if housework is relatively low on her list of priorities, she is likely to resent them for keeping her from preferred activities. Even if the company is generous with its relocation allowances, the couple may find that they have cash flow problems at this stage. Worries that they may not be able to balance their accounts in the long run (because they have taken on too high a mortgage, perhaps) are an added pressure. Even ordinary day-to-day activities can be made more difficult in these first months because the wife has the added task of mapping out the new locality. She must find the best stores from which to buy basic commodities, contact the providers of necessary services and locate a wide range of important facilities.

Her second main task will be to do anything she can to help her children adjust, watching their progress with concern. How well they settle in at school (especially if they have to cope with curriculum changes) and how quickly they make new friends will be the main determinants of success. Most mobile parents felt that their children were more adaptable, and good at making friends, than the norm, although there were reports of some who were shy and found moving disturbing. Mothers, especially, wait eagerly for the first signs of integration—getting involved in after-school activities, bringing friends home, going out in the evenings, etc.—and often try to

142

speed the process by contacting mothers of potential play-mates.

While the family's needs usually come first, the wife must devote some energy to starting a new life for herself. An initial period of loneliness appears to be almost inevitable. Moving means a complete disruption of her identity (Seidenberg, 1972). While husband and children carry over stability areas—job, school, home life—the woman must face changes on all fronts. Many of the sample commented on the overwhelming newness of suddenly finding oneself in a new place: "the house doesn't feel as if it's mine," "when I go shopping I don't know anyone," "I just can't settle down to do anything," "suddenly there's nothing." Reactions to this feeling and actions to cope with it vary widely and appear to be as much related to personality and initial favorableness to moving as to objective characteristics of the situation. Some wives become overwhelmed and depressed, failing to respond even when things go their way, whereas others believe that this is a necessary phase and that they should take the initiative in getting to know the area and introducing themselves to potential contacts.

Although individual factors of perception play a large part in determining the wife's reaction to her new environment, situational factors can have profound effects either to accentuate or attenuate feelings of loneliness at this time. Circumstances which were quoted as accentuating loneliness can be grouped under three headings:

1. Those which isolate her from her past—leaving behind close friends, for example.

143

2. Those which make her feel isolated from her present—not liking available organized activities, her husband working long hours, finding herself in distanced suburbia when she prefers the city (or vice versa).

3. Those which isolate her from what she considers to be potentially acceptable futures—being tied to the house by young children, living in an isolated town. Hope would appear to be a major factor here; having no friends in a new community is not as demoralizing as the feeling that one is in a poor position to make the kind of friends one would like.

Many wives described their reactions to these dismal first months: the way they wandered around alone, went shopping too often or looked forward to the mail delivery —anything in an attempt to relieve the loneliness. In retrospect most agreed that settling in is usually a gradual process which must be approached with patience and determination; they were, however, grateful for any situational factors which made this period easier. Experienced mobiles might move to a modern housing development where they know that they will find people of their own kind. The baby-sitting and car-sharing clubs and "welcome wagons" which are currently proliferating in such communities are an organized way of making contacts if not friends. The children help a great deal, both by keeping her occupied and by acting as an introduction to other parents. Being befriended by a neighbor or another company wife can also play an important part in easing these early pressures.

The manager's wife's happiness will depend on how successful she is in these three main task areas and will, in its turn, affect the amount of social support she is able to give her husband. If she is coping well, she will do her best to provide him, too, with a stable home background, arrange a few social engagements to introduce him to her newfound acquaintances and be open to discuss, should he want to do so, any problems he is having at work. If, instead, she is unhappy for her own or her children's sake, she may direct her anger (resentment? misery?) toward him at a time when he has little spare capacity to deal with interpersonal difficulties. The manager is, then, as vulnerable after as during moving to secondhand stress from his wife. She is likely to be responsive, in her turn, to his moods. If he is unhappy with his new job or develops a poor relationship with his superior, subordinates or colleagues, he may bring his disappointment home. If either or both parties feel that they have made a mistake about the move in general or any particular aspect (the new house and its location), they are likely to be fainthearted in their efforts to start a new life and may end up living in limbo until called upon to move again.

Settling in takes time. Most couples would agree that moving takes a year out of your life. After six months together in the new location the family is relatively established. The house is organized and familiar and able to provide the security necessary of a home. The manager has reached the stage when his new job shows signs of

145

being mastered. His wife and children have made friends, joined clubs, etc., and are on their way to becoming members of the local community. There we shall leave them as we turn to a brief consideration of two of the many important variables which intervene to affect experiences of this event.

VARIATIONS ON THE BASIC PATTERN

Having spotlighted the average managerial family, we should like to conclude this chapter by looking at variations on the basic pattern. Again (as in chapter 5), life stage and the role the manager's wife adopts are the main dimensions of variance. Both are particularly appropriate to the theme of this chapter: having so far considered time as governing the dynamic evolution of a potentially stressful event, we shall now go on to discuss it, firstly as the aging process of the family and, secondly, of society.

Variations with Life Stage

Life stage is a complex variable—amalgamating age, marital status, number and age of children, etc.—which has proved especially helpful to those studying variations in the demands on and resources of the family as a unit (e.g., Wells and Gubar, 1966, on family expenditure patterns). It is no surprise, then, that it appears as a critical factor explaining the predominance of certain relocation problems at certain times. It is important to note that in the summary of trends which follows, it is likely to also

146

stand for the number of previous relocations since this was closely associated with age for the sample studied.

The Single Manager

Moving has its problems for the single man but these are few compared to those at later life stages. His main concern is the job and being seen to do well in it (at a critical and well-watched phase). Other potential pressures are the culture shock of starting work after life at college, having no separate world to retire to in the evenings to relax, the problems of house hunting, being lonely in a strange town (often peopled mainly by married couples) and trying to maintain contact with old friends (including a possible future wife?). On the other hand, moving around has considerable benefits. It provides an opportunity to see new places as well as to gain experience which will stand him in good stead in the future.

The Young Married

With marriage, moving usually becomes easier as the manager now has someone with whom to share the tasks, disappointments and successes involved. Even living in a disliked area of the country is tolerated if there are compensations and the stay is not seen as being for life. Again, the manager's job dominates. The new pattern (see chapter 5) of his wife continuing to work means that she is less likely to suffer the loneliness which was the preceding generation's main problem. This is usually an active and satisfying time for the couple socially, as well as a busy one for those who enjoy home improving and decorating.

147

Married with a Young Family

House hunting now becomes a major problem both because the wife is too tied down to participate much and because house choice becomes more crucial and criteria more exacting. Size, nearness to schools and stores and, as the wife is now housebound, potential friends must all be considered. Separation, which because of the practical problems involved usually lasts longer than at earlier life stages, is an emotionally draining time for all the family. The wife's adaptation to and happiness in her new environment become critical factors. The couple find it harder to make out-of-work friends, tied down as they are, and more emphasis is placed on nearness (the neighbors) and acquaintances in a similar situation (e.g., couples with children of the same age and interests). Housing can be a vital factor here and many choose to live in modern housing developments where they can be with their own kind. Area of the country is also important; being unable to feel at home in a particular region can make settling down more difficult.

Preschool children are relatively no problem to move compared to those over five years old for whom education becomes important. Having to arrange schooling now becomes a major factor and for many this is the main determining factor of house location and the timing of the move.

The manager's job while sometimes unsatisfactory is usually as much a stabilizing as a disruptive factor in moving. It gives him something to do during the day, provides a ready-made system of contacts and potential friends and opens substantial opportunities for achievement and satisfaction. Compared to this his wife is at a considerable disadvantage and has to start from scratch to build a new life. Most managers agree that it is she who bears the brunt of moving.

At this stage relocation is welcomed more for its long- than its short-term advantages; the manager's promotion, moving to a better house, improving a previously unsatisfactory situation and getting out of a rut are some of its more frequently quoted benefits. If moves come too frequently, as they sometimes do at this formative career stage, this can, in itself, be a source of stress (especially to the wife) irrespective of the particular details. Couples begin to develop strategies to cope with repeated disruptions. Packard (1972) suggests that American managers and their wives become adept at "instant gregariousness."

Married with a Teenage Family

Moving now affects the fates of (say) four, rather than two, adult individuals, all of whom will probably become actively involved in the initial decision. The manager, though, as chief breadwinner usually retains the casting vote. He and his wife are now only repeating familiar, if at times still painful, procedures and their main concern will be the satisfaction of their children's needs. Continuity of schooling and losing and making friends are the most critical factors. Relocation

149

difficulties can make adolescence an even more turbulent time than would normally be expected. Often teenagers react with resentment and rebellion at the thought of moving, especially if they have lived long enough in one place to think of it as home, with all the word implies. Usually, though, they settle down relatively easily in the new community and appear to benefit from a lesson in adaptability.

The Empty Nest

Most of those who are still moving at this life stage have come to regard mobility as an acceptable and natural way of life. It is likely to be a sign that the manager is successful in his job and this will be a source of satisfaction to both partners. They may find that repeated moving has prevented them from becoming (and discouraged them from wanting to become) involved in the local communities through which they have passed. It will, however, also have given them friends all over the country, so that they seldom have to start from scratch in establishing the level of contact they do desire. Many do express some concern that they never settle down anywhere and that they are not providing a stable focus for their, now also mobile, children and grandchildren to refer to and visit. Where to retire to becomes a problem for those who have lived in so many places but belonged to none.

Table 6.1 summarizes the conclusions of this section, showing the predominant problems at each of the various life stages.

Moving with a Career-Oriented Wife: A Glimpse into the Future

The average manager has a wife whose main concerns are to see to his and their children's comforts and look after the home. In chapter 5 we suggested that theirs is a declining marriage pattern; we shall, then, conclude this chapter with a brief consideration of what relocation may mean to the new generation, the aspiring dual-career family.

Mobility in phase with the husband's career progress

Table 6.1
PREDOMINANT RELOCATION PROBLEMS AT DIFFERENT LIFE STAGES

| | Single | Married | | |
		No children	Young children	Older children	Empty Nest
The job	x				
Separation from family			x		
Housing			x	x	
Wife's reluctance to move			x	x	
Wife's adaptation to new environment		x	x		
Children				x	x
Education			x	x	
Responsibilities to parents					x
Social life		x		x	

makes it almost impossible for the wife to develop a working life of her own. She will have difficulty seeing any necessary training courses through to the end, may have to leave a job she enjoys and have to start again at the bottom of the ladder elsewhere and often finds that there are no jobs in her field in the new location. Having to mark time for six months or so while she sees to the chores of moving is both an added aggravation and makes her even less desirable as a prospective employee when she is free to look for work. (A further negative qualification at this stage is that she cannot guarantee she will not soon be moved again.) A previous safe bet in such trying circumstances was teaching. It was eminently transferable and also, by nature, part time, fitting in well with commitments to the rest of the family. This is no longer such an easy option; not only have qualification requirements become more rigorous, but there are now few vacancies in the profession.

So what can the manager's wife do? At the moment she has three basic options. The first is to decide that her husband's job comes first and fit any work opportunities she has around its requirements, probably hoping to return to full-time employment at a later, more stable life stage. She may, in the meantime, divert her energies to being a housewife and mother and casual voluntary work. At the other extreme is the wife who succeeds in developing her own career. There are currently very few who come into this category, although it is on the increase (Rapoport and Rapoport, 1976). Rapoport and Rapoport describe some of the elaborate support systems dual-career families need to be able to maintain their chosen life-style; an almost essential ingredient is that the husband should stay in one place. Today's young executives are reported to be much less willing than previous generations to move within companies (although we have seen no official figures to support this); having to satisfy their wives' as well as their own career needs is likely to be one of the main reasons behind this trend. Between those two pure options comes the third, the broad band of compromise. Many couples are trying to achieve the best of both worlds, letting the man's promotion opportunities (perhaps in the future it will even be the woman's) dictate their pattern of movement but looking for a satisfying job for the wife in each new location. This is by no means easy, especially as the wife must usually start from scratch in each position (her husband's within-company transfer is more of a progression), usually after a break from work in which she has been busy moving. Today's young mobile wife is in the same relationship to her job that her predecessor was to her home and social life: for both, relocation means a disruptive end and a traumatic beginning. If she adds mother to her repertoire of roles, the manager's wife stands even less chance of achieving any work ambitions she may have. Her husband is in a difficult, ambivalent position in this respect; while he may well sympathize with her problems, he is likely to be extremely conscious of the benefits to him, firstly, of relocation (for the promotion, new job challenge, etc., it brings) and, secondly, of her being forced into the supportive housewife role.

It is interesting to speculate where current trends will lead. Their immediate consequences seem to be an increasing number of childless marriages (Farid, 1974,

153

reports a postponement of starting their families or adding to them and a decline in mean ultimate family size for women married since 1964) and a growing number of young managers who are less than wholly dedicated to the companies they work for (and to working per se?) and place a compensatingly greater emphasis on having a satisfying family life and helping their wives satisfy their own career needs. As men and women experiment with their own and each other's roles, the balance of power is shifting, not only within the family, but also within the companies which employ its members. Male managers seem to be setting themselves lower ambitions, while their wives strive to fill three highly demanding roles simultaneously. Companies with an eye to the future must keep abreast of these developments if they are to retain the loyalty of their employees and know what rewards to offer in the future, and *to whom.*

7

COPING WITH STRESS

It will be the underlying tenet of this chapter that interventions to cope with stress can be of three rather different types: they can be retrospective, either (1) to remedy populationwide stressors or (2) to cope with individually defined stress as it occurs, or prospective, (3) to prevent stress. All three types should be based on company-specific diagnosis of the causes of stress, the characteristics of the individuals concerned, the company norms and values and any other factors which influence which specific coping strategies are appropriate and who should be the initiating actor(s). The first half of the chapter will be devoted to a consideration of these three types of intervention: we shall first consider ways of tackling stress at the level of the individual (i.e., when it is triggered by a particular configuration of $P:E$ elements at a particular point in time), then look at possible remedies for stressors that are known to have ill effects for large sectors of the managerial population and finally go on to discuss the possible prevention of stress. In the second half we shall turn our attention to the chief of the company's stress reduction actors—the personnel officer.

Before considering possible actions to deal with current stresses or to prevent their future development, a note of caution: It has been found (Marshall and Cooper, 1976) that pressures and satisfactions are closely linked facets of the manager's job. Few, if any, job areas can be identified as purely a source of one or the other for the population as a whole, for the manager over time (short-term stress is frequently a prelude to satisfaction) or even for the individual at an instant in time. In attempting to remove known causes of stress from the work environment, we could face the danger of either (1) generating different pressures (worker participation while alleviating alienation at blue collar levels is, for example, putting added burdens on many managers) *or* (2) reducing job satisfaction (the growth-inducing potential of stress must particularly not be forgotten). Organizationwide reform, then, must be undertaken only with extreme caution and always be based on meaningful subgroup diagnosis and cater to individual needs. On whatever scale action is planned it should always incorporate the facility for modification, even complete reversal, if this becomes necessary in the light of feedback about its effects (from its own self-monitoring). The aim, in short, should be not to eradicate stress but to *manage* it. Stress management *need not be a discontinuity*—the idea that it might be helps to frighten higher management whenever it is suggested; it is already part and parcel of management training, organizational development, even work study—anything which is geared toward improving the various dimensions of organizational life.

COPING WITH STRESS AT THE LEVEL OF THE INDIVIDUAL

Stress is a result of the dynamic interaction of individual with environment and is triggered by the former's perception of threat (Lazarus, 1967). It is then that vulnerability, stressors and context come together (Maclean, 1976). In line with this view, Figure 7.1 depicts the dynamic development of a stress situation, which is taken here as a basis for the discussion of retrospective intervention at the level of the individual. Initially, a particular combination of pressures is identified as stressful by the individual: he feels anxious, unable to cope and displays his characteristic pattern of physical and mental symptoms of stress and defensive behavior. This is the period of "shock" described by Lazarus (1967) in his four-stage model of stress, during which the individual builds up strength to face the future. The behavior which follows this period of "protective withdrawal" can be categorized as either adaptive or maladaptive, depending on the consequences it has for the individual concerned (and subsequently his colleagues, organization, family, etc.). Adaptive behavior deals directly with the stressful situation by seeking and implementing solutions; it not only does away with the current problems but also prepares the individual to deal with similar situations in the future,

157

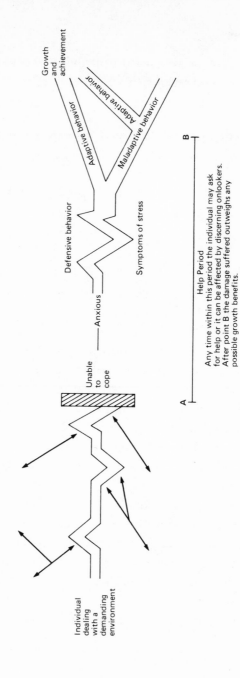

Figure 7.1 Dynamic representation of a stress situation showing the individual's behavioral alternatives

and can lead to a well-earned sense of achievement. Adaptive behavior is, therefore, developmental. Maladaptive behavior, on the other hand, does not deal directly with the problem; it is self-protective and while it may remove the stress situation is only likely to do so temporarily. It frequently does not dissipate the anxiety felt by the individual and does not help him to cope with similar future situations. (Using such a definition, prevention of the development of stress can also be said to have maladaptive consequences in the wider context of the individual's future satisfaction and growth, and the organization's ability to cope successfully with its environment.) In Figure 7.1 we have hypothesized that maladaptive behavior can profitably become adaptive any time up to point B, after which the negative consequences (psychological distress, disruption of work performance and relationships, etc.) cannot be compensated for by the possible benefits of ultimate successful coping.

The management of stress should be concerned with how this switch (from maladaptive to adaptive behavior) can be achieved, who should be involved and what actions are appropriate. The view presented here is that the onus is on the individual concerned but that he cannot cope without organizational support.

When should intervention take place? In the figure we have designated a help period ending at point B. Up to this point the damage caused to any of the parties is minimal, the psychological tension felt by the individual concerned is likely to be an impetus to, and a necessary precondition of, growth and achievement. It is only if maladaptive behavior follows point B that permanent

159

damage becomes a probability; it is here, therefore, that intervention is appropriate. Intervention is used to mean initiative to treat the situation as a problem rather than to pretend that it is manageable within already established work routines. This initiative may come from one of three groups of actors; these groups can be distinguished in terms of both the directness of their relationship with the problem situation and also their ability to intervene effectively. At the focus of the situation is the individual concerned—only he has full information as to what are the sources of stress (having defined them as such himself). The most immediate and effective action can be expected if he asks for help. If, however, the individual concerned avoids admitting his feelings, it may be necessary for someone close to him to recognize the situation and to take action. These are people who relate directly to the individual (his boss, colleagues, wife) and who thus should have some idea as to what his overall circumstances are and how he is coping with them. In many cases the problem is not in fact dealt with until members of the third group of people, outsiders, have become involved (company doctors, counselors or higher level managers to whose attention unsatisfactory work, poor health, etc., has been brought).

It is best, for many reasons, if the initiative comes from the individual under stress, for action is more immediate, loss of self-esteem is less probable, the situation is not likely to have developed to an unmanageable stage, etc. The *management of stress* should be concerned with making this outcome the most likely.

A necessary prerequisite to answering the question

"How can this be done?" is to understand why so many people suffer stress in comparative silence. Many possible reasons suggest themselves, but these can be grouped into four main categories:

1. Lack of awareness on the part of the manager.
2. Personality characteristics which make only high involvement in work satisfying.
3. Career ambitions.
4. Probably the most important, fear of external sanctions—from the company, colleagues and, possibly, people outside the organization too, if he disconfirms their image of him.

Again we see that to be adequate the explanation must include both person and environment factors in interaction. Unless there are changes in both systems, opportunities for coping will not be improved. Once the individual recognizes his need to cope with stress (self-awareness is a necessary but not always easy first step), three broad strategies are open to him: these are, in order of their magnitude of effect, discussion, negotiation and action to change.

It is probably difficult to admit one's inability to cope in the actual work situation (it is there that the most damage can be done), and so we can draw up a hierarchy of situations in which the manager can discuss his problems in order of the formers' potential threat. As discussion of a problem is often sufficient to prompt the individual to find his own solution or to view it as of less importance, opportunities for frank discussion should be maximized.

The least threatening confidants are those outside work, probably the manager's wife and possibly his doctor; while these may provide substantial emotional support, they lack the work expertise from which to suggest and participate in appropriate solutions. For this reason the manager may choose to turn for advice to relatively nonthreatening levels of his organization, the company doctor, the personnel officer, a colleague or a counseling service, if provided. (The latter is a suggestion for the future rather than a reality of today.) It is precisely if the manager turns directly to those involved (boss, colleagues or subordinates) in the problem situation (in such cases negotiating as well as discussing) that the manager makes himself the most vulnerable, but it is at this level that he can expect to have the maximum effect. If it is necessary at all, action is usually a natural development of previous discussion and negotiation. Support and change may, however, be required of those around him if the manager is to achieve a long-term solution to his problem.

Two basic needs, therefore, emerge: the first is for an organizational atmosphere and structure in which the employee feels he is free to express his inability to cope, discuss his fears and ask for help; the second is for an individual who is aware of his need to do these things and be able to communicate meaningfully.

Training courses for individuals, or work teams, can go a long way toward meeting the latter, while company policy (backed up by company action) will be a major determinant of the former. Ideally, the company should aim to develop an organizational structure and work pattern which foster good communications, openness and trust; it will then encourage the manager to cope with his stress publicly and adaptively rather than privately and defensively.

In many companies today the prevailing norm (that one should never show signs of stress) will not be easily or quickly changed and even a friendly personnel officer or a counseling service may be too threatening to be of immediate use. If this is the case, the company itself can take on the responsibility, hopefully temporary, of looking for even individual-specific stress and appropriately helping the individuals or work groups concerned. The proactive behavioral scientist "troubleshooter" needed for such a task would not find *his* role easy, but once such a strategy had shown positive results and affected company norms in the direction of openness, he would soon become unnecessary.

COPING WITH ORGANIZATIONAL (ENVIRONMENTAL) SOURCES OF STRESS

Our discussion so far has been very general and has avoided identifying particular P or E elements it would be desirable to change. Recurring themes in this book have, however, suggested that there are some common stressors in the environment against which more specific remedial action might beneficially be taken.

Work Overload

Restriction of work load from above is not, practically or ethically, a feasible solution for managers. It is particularly undesirable since one of the main benefits of being a manager is having a wide unspecified work load within which to create one's own job. Ways must, therefore, be found of discouraging the individual from taking on more than he can cope with. Individual training can help here, especially if it develops skills which foster the abilities to delegate and to assess in advance the need for, and afterward ensure efficient use of, work done. Superiors too can contribute by showing awareness of, and sympathy for, their subordinates' capacities, and respecting the motivations of those who wish to lead a balanced life. The company for its part can make a realistic assessment of the work to be done, ensuring adequate staffing levels and trying not to unfairly favor those who overwork (whose lack of control/balance may well be a danger in the long run). But above all, company norms must adapt to make open negotiation of work load possible and sensible rather than maximum performance respectable.

As the concept of company norms will be used repeatedly, a brief consideration of their nature, source and impact is appropriate here. Norms (social) are, in this context, "standards of behavior developed by members of a group to which they conform or are encouraged to comply with by penalties" (Eysenck, Arnold and Meili, 1972). They arise and evolve within the organization rather than being explicitly formulated (by company or employees) and are closely linked to underlying values. As the stan-

164

dards by which acceptable versus unacceptable is judged, they are a vital part of organizational life. Norms are open to both informal and formal influence, but the former, the influence by which they mainly develop, appears to have the greater power. It is not sufficient for the company to state that rejection of promotion does not jeopardize future prospects; this must be seen by managers to be true before the company myth on this issue loses its power to influence behavior. Communication is the main medium of influence—the discovery alone, that most other managers are not *in fact* coping effortlessly, for example, could well have a major impact on attitudes and, eventually, behavior.

Reduction of work load is, then, a joint responsibility of employer and employee. Though the former is in an appropriate position to initiate change, the task is essentially that of achieving a new balance between them at a lower level of company expectations : employee input.

Lack of Autonomy

Feeling pressured by a lack of autonomy is partly an inevitable consequence of working for a company, but especially one of any size. Managers on the whole realize that they are trading their freedom for the high pay, security and wide range of job and career opportunities the company offer, but this realization does not always make the situation emotionally acceptable. For his part the individual should, therefore, recognize his contribution to the frustrating conflict situation in which he finds himself and, if he is not willing to take the risk of leaving, do his best

165

to accommodate to those aspects of company member-ship which are no more than realities of organizational life. This is not to suggest that improvements in the over-all situation cannot be made. Worker participation is a vogue movement at the current time and may have a role to play even at managerial levels. Managers frequently report that being allowed greater independence by their immediate boss and to have one's say are a major source of job satisfaction, which suggests that much can be achieved at the level of the immediate superior : subordi-nate interaction. The fostering of good communications within an organization can also help by keeping em-ployees in touch with decisions even if they have little power to influence them. These suggestions are appropri-ate to the manager in his subordinate role. Restricted opportunities for independence are also a result of his middle-man position: he is under pressure from below as well as above. The manager's role in relation to the gen-eral work force is currently in a state of flux, with the latter demanding greater participation and, in effect, threatening the former's power and status. Some of the stress labeled as lack of autonomy reflects a confusion (and disappointment) about eroded status, both at work and in the wider context of society, with which the middle-class manager has still to learn to cope. It is somewhat artificial to consider the two vertical arms of the manager's rela-tionships with other company members separately. Sup-port from above becomes particularly important when one's position is challenged from below. In the reverse direction, good relationships with subordinates can be jeopardized if the manager is not given enough information—about their future career opportunities or job security, for example—to be able to deal openly with them. While it will be interesting to see at what state worker: manager: higher management relationships stabilize, the period of transition we are now witnessing must be acknowledged as one of high potential stressfulness for all concerned.

Career Development Pressures

A dominant theme which appears in managerial stress literature (e.g., Buck, 1972; Wagstaff, 1976) is career development. While there are, obviously, individual variations, it is possible to chart the general trend of a company's requirements of its managers and of the latters' work motivations over their life cycles. This was done in detail in chapter 4, and here Figure 7.2 summarizes the trends described.

Mismatch between expectations/hopes and achievements can be a major source of frustration and stress. Both the analysis presented here and that of Guest and Williams (1973), which brings together the demands of the manager's work and home systems at different stages of the life cycle, suggest that careers will be particularly problematic to two age groups—the aspiring young and the middle-aged manager. The one is at a time of maximum job involvement and the other is facing a more general life crisis. If this is so, the young manager's stress, if any, is largely the result of self-imposed pressure (albeit partly determined by his perception of external reality), whereas the older manager appears to be more at the

Figure 7.2

COMPANY EXPECTATIONS VERSUS REWARDS
OFFERED DURING THE LIFE OF THE AVERAGE
MANAGER

	Company expectations	Rewards	Employees' reactions
Young Managers	Demand flexibility, mobility and high levels of job involvement.	High levels of pay, experience, rapid promotion, a wider range of career prospects.	Tension and conflict but high levels of job satisfaction. Above average anxiety scores.
Middle-aged Managers	Continuing job involvement. A greater emphasis is placed on performing well in, rather than just mastering, each job.	Stability, some steady progress based on past achievements. Fewer promotion opportunities.	Considerable satisfaction. Some disappointment and reappraisal later on.
Older Managers	No longer requires total dedication. Demands competence rather than contribution.	Even fewer opportunities for promotion. Sideways or even downward job moves may be necessary.	Some adapt and seek satisfaction outside work. Others fail to adapt, cannot escape feelings of failure and frustration. Above average anxiety scores.

mercy of external forces. Job satisfaction (on the career-development dimension) would, then, appear to be for the young, the established middle-aged manager, the very lucky (those who are boardroom material) and the philosophical (those who accept and accommodate to having reached their career ceilings). Disappointment and frustration in later life are, in fact, inevitable consequences of a work environment in which all other job satisfactions are subservient to that of promotion. The young manager learns to accept a job not because he will necessarily enjoy it or reap benefits from doing it well but because it is promotion and so that he will merit the next step up. The company's reward structure (which reflects the value of this population subgroup) encourages this attitude toward work. If he uses the same yardstick of success and aims for the same goals, the older manager is by the very nature of things vulnerable to frustration. Thwarted ambition is frequently the major job pressure for older managers, and concern about career development the major concern of their younger colleagues.

How can this situation be improved? The tax man has already acted to reduce the attraction of promotion by minimizing its monetary benefits especially at top management levels. For its part the organization could possibly help to shift the emphasis of achievement from status to autonomy and growth within a job by modifying its reward structures. It should also consider how it copes with its middle management bulge and look for alternative management development strategies to that of exciting and then snubbing a large number of its personnel. In this respect some organizations are better placed than others: banks, for example, have more top jobs than industrial firms and so can offer ultimate career success to more of their employees. The employee must, however, take much of the responsibility for handling his own development. He must learn to appraise the situation and his capabilities realistically and either plan for the long term (i.e., appreciate that the organization is not going to want

169

his whole dedication for ever) or be prepared to accommodate to short-term changes (or temporary fluctuations) in work demands. Mismatch is a two-party problem and must, therefore, be attacked on both fronts; frank employee evaluation procedures, an accepted opportunity for confrontation, can make a substantial contribution to the good feeling of all concerned.

PREVENTION OF JOB STRESS

In reality it is only if we can foresee, rather than simply react to, stress that we can plan its prevention rather than cater to its speedy cure. Bearing in mind the role of pressure as an impetus to growth and a source of satisfaction, in those situations in which stress is defined individually (by a particular P : E combination at a particular time) the latter technique is adequate to prevent individuals developing long-term stress reactions. Suitable interventions have been discussed above and suggest that preventative measures open to organizations should concentrate on two aspects: developing the individual so that he can diagnose and handle his own stress, and creating an atmosphere in which he is able to do so constructively. The individual's responsibility is to exploit to the full the opportunities he is thus offered. Four broad strategies for achieving these goals are open to an organization: design of organizational structure, job design, personnel selection and placement, and training.

Job Design

Job design acts on the environment side of the P : E equation. From both empirical and qualitative studies we find combinations of job factors which can be identified as intrinsically stressful. These can mainly be explained as resulting either from conflicting demands (e.g., the need for research managers to be both scientists and good managers) or facets of company structure (e.g., the "boxed-in" middle manager). An organization in which there are impossible positions has a duty to its employees to either change them or adapt interlocking systems to alleviate their effects.

Design of Organizational Structure and Atmosphere

For most companies organizational structure is already fixed. Many do, however, plan its modification via organizational development programs in which improved communications and participation are two of the main ways of enhancing employee satisfaction adopted. Showing concern is, in fact, the critical step as it directly affects company atmosphere and company norms: trust and openness are as important influences on employee performance (if not more so for those at managerial level) as physical working conditions. Even in imperfect conditions there are still ways (listening to and being ready to act on employees' suggestions or problems, for example) in which higher management can, if genuinely interested, improve the quality of organizational life.

Personnel Selection and Placement

Turning to the other side of the P : E fit equation, the company can select which individuals it chooses to employ and can take care to place them in positions appropriate to their abilities and experience. Selection is usually in terms of basic demographic details (although even in this area choice is not a simple matter—the firm may not always need the fit and the young, or be able to utilize the skills of the well qualified). But do research results suggest that personality screening should also be carried out? If the traits required to perform a particular job well are known, selection can obviously help in achieving a good P : E fit (allowing a margin of error for the accuracy of the test used and the admissible range of scores) and can, therefore, be of mutual benefit to both company and employee. Personality and interests tests are already widely used for this purpose but tend to concentrate on the skills aspects of profiles. If, however, the intention is to consider emotional make-up and select out stress-prone individuals, both practical and ethical problems arise:

1. The literature reveals at least two personality types particularly vulnerable to stress—the anxious and the ambitious. Managers of the latter type (if not both types) are likely to possess characteristics that make them valued organizational members.
2. In order to be able to select out (say) anxiety-prone individuals, we must be able to accurately identify them. As anxiety is largely situational (i.e., only

appears under pressure), this may be a difficult task open to considerable experimental error.

3. Anxiety is a *natural* reaction to environmental pressure and, up to a certain level, results in adaptive responses, probably in improved work performance. It would, therefore, be against the company's interests to be staffed by personnel who did not react in this way. (Some jobs do involve exceptionally high levels of pressure and it might be appropriate to select, for these, individuals with a high stress tolerance.)

4. Stress-prone individuals will react (and incur harm) in any appropriate stimulus situation. Is it the company's or their own responsibility to decide what levels of stress they are willing to tolerate? Research (Marshall, 1977) indicates that refusing job challenges to employees can also act to increase their stress.

We must conclude, then, that it would be practically difficult and probably misguided to base personnel selection on stress-prone personality profiles, although these may be of value in guiding placement in certain instances.

Training

Skills training (e.g., in the use of inflation accounting techniques) fills an obvious need and helps the individual perform well in his job. Other techniques which are much more dependent on personal relevance (e.g., T-groups, transcendental meditation, transactional analysis, etc.)

have as their aims personal growth, often with an emphasis on interpersonal skills. These can play a considerable (if immeasurable) part in fitting the individual to cope with pressures in and derive satisfaction from both his work and home lives. A recent development in this field has been that of courses specifically designed to help individuals cope with stress (e.g., Burns, 1976). While many of the proposed techniques focus on symptoms (some, for example, are borrowed from behavior therapy), attention is also paid to self-diagnosis of the causes of stress (Wright, 1975b, for example, makes soundly practical suggestions in this area).

The individual manager can also participate in the prevention of stress by:

1. Making sure that he is placed in a job suitable to his characteristics and talents
2. Putting effort into achieving a balance between himself and his job, his work and his family which is acceptable and practical
3. Facing up realistically to what he can and cannot achieve in terms of career development
4. Taking every opportunity to develop his powers to prevent and/or cope with stress so that he can improve the quality of his life at work and at home
5. Fostering relationships which help him cope with work pressure and admit and remedy work stress. Marshall's (1977) study looked very much at the manager *on his own,* and it was therefore possible to assess the role of social

support in coping in the context of only one (but perhaps the most important) relationship, that with his wife. It was evident from her interview data that the wife's support made a vital contribution to his ability to control stress. Social support in coping in the workplace could be an even more effective tool.

Altogether in this chapter three broad strategies for coping with stress in an organization have been outlined; these are summarized in Figure 7.3. Since stress has been shown to be caused multi-factorially, its management, then, must be approached simultaneously on several fronts.

THE SCOPE FOR THE PERSONNEL INITIATIVE

We have already suggested much that the individual can do to help himself and ways in which higher management, particularly his immediate superior (overworked though he, too, probably is) can help in a day-to-day context. Further organizational initiatives to assist stressed managers and others at work may come from a number of sources, but the personnel officer, by virtue of his role and expertise, is the one most likely to succeed within the organization. We should like here to consider Torrington and Cooper's (1977) suggestions as to the range of interventions that could come from personnel specialists

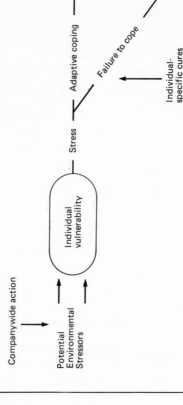

PREVENTION

Organizational structure design
Job Design
Personnel Selection and Placement
Training
   of the manager both in his roles as
      individual and superior
   and of work teams

CURE (based on company-specific diagnosis)

Companywide Action

It may be possible to identify certain companywide stressors which can be tackled at an overall level. Poor morale, lack of job security, and restricted career opportunities are likely to be among those of managers in any company today.

Companywide action

Potential
Environmental
Stressors

Individual
vulnerability

Stress

Adaptive coping

Failure to cope

Individual-
specific cures

Individual-Specific Action

Much job stress is due to the interaction of a specific individual with a specific job context at a particular point in time and *cannot be foreseen*. Action must, therefore, be concerned with making sure that it is followed as soon as possible by effective coping.

Figure 7.3 Broad strategies for managing stress in an organization

within an organization.* They are grouped under two headings:

Operational: These are strategies modifying existing personnel operations to take account of their potential for stress mitigation

Influential: These refer to the potential for stress mitigation secondhand, through the influence of personnel specialists on overall management philosophy and policy

Operational 1: Performance Review

The current trend in performance appraisal is to move away from the judgment of a boss on the performance of a subordinate toward a discussion between colleagues about the progress of a job in which they both have an interest: one as the job holder and the other as being responsible for the performance of the job holder. Among others, Beveridge (1974) and Randell et al. (1972) have identified this trend and expounded its method. Personnel officers monitoring performance review programs and coaching managers in interview methods could incorporate an element of stress identification in the procedures they advocate. Beveridge's approach is particularly susceptible to this type of development as the job holder is encouraged to identify and comment upon the prob-

*The material that follows was published by one of the authors (C.L. Cooper) with D. Torrington in an article entitled "The Management of Stress and the Personnel Initiative" in *Personnel Review*, 1977.

177

lems standing in the way of effective performance. An interviewer with the requisite skill and sensitivity may enable the interviewee at least to engage in catharsis, with the possibility of going further by helping to work out adaptive behaviors for the job holder to initiate or to encourage stress-relieving initiatives within the organizational context in which the job is done.

The potential dangers of this approach are the temptation of the interviewer to play God, or to seek out personal problems of the interviewee as a convenient reason for unsatisfactory performance, which neatly absolve the interviewer from taking any action or bearing any responsibility. Notwithstanding these hazards, the performance review still provides an opportunity for stress identification, as it is an occasion when matters are being discussed in a manner more detached and reflective than in most interactive encounters at work.

Operational 2: The Professional Counselor

An alternative may lie in the work of the small number of people employed in organizations in a quasi-professional counseling capacity. Occasionally, an organization will have in its ranks a professional psychologist whose job is to be available to discuss personal problems with employees. His services could be extremely helpful in providing a means toward stress mitigation for individuals. The problem lies in the reluctance of the individual to be seen seeking such assistance, and it may be more effective if the expert masquerades under a title like welfare officer or even management development officer, whose advice could be sought without necessarily being seen as acknowledging a personal psychological impairment. A similar type of function could, however, be exercised by at least two other professionals who feature in some organizations: the doctor and the industrial chaplain, both of whom have the great advantage of being perceived as independent of the organization and its decision-making processes and thus as people not likely to weaken an employee's career prospects. Both are seen as appropriate repositories of confidences and as sources of two kinds of solace—medication or spiritual guidance—beyond the capacity of the organization.

A study of executive health care (1971) indicated that only 5 percent of companies having health care schemes included psychiatric counseling as part of the scheme, but this referred only to organizations actually employing a psychiatrist specifically for this purpose. The survey included the comment:

> . . . if one believes that managers need health care primarily because of the stress of their work, then this would be a useful adjunct to a normal checkup, and many doctors do include this as part of the regular medical checkup.

If counseling on stress is available from the doctor on demand, then it may well produce the type of inhibition already described for other possible initiatives, but an established practice of regular health checks on executives sets up a cycle of encounters in which there is the possibility of stress being discussed. There are the addi-

179

tional obvious advantages that the doctor will be able to diagnose a wider range of stress symptoms than other potential interveners as well as being able to infer stress proneness from a medical history. It is beyond our competence to consider the place of medication in mitigating stress, but if it is appropriate, only the doctor, within the organization, can provide it.

The survey showed the chaplains' activities to be mainly directed toward the needs of blue collar workers rather than managers. Nevertheless, they are perceived as being neutral and they carry out their duties principally by walking around and talking to people without arousing too much suspicion about their motives. Like the doctor, their training and vocation has familiarized them with the counseling role and the revelation of people's deep fears and anxieties. Here, potentially, is another source of external intervention.

Operational 3: Training

A third area of operations, usually under the control of the personnel specialists, is training and, again, there are stress-relieving possibilities. The purpose of training courses is to aid the operational performance of course attenders when they return to their normal role and, if the course succeeds in this, it is likely to reduce stress proneness by increasing the feeling of competence and confidence that the trainee has in relation to his work. Also, the course extracts a person from his normal work environment for a period in which he is relieved of the normal pressures of his duties, with the opportunity to reflect upon them, discuss them with others and, potentially, set them in a more healthy perspective. Both of these are built into almost any course.

Certain features of training could be considered to deal with stress symptoms more directly. The first is sensitivity training, which is a method of enabling people to see themselves as others see them, by stripping away cultural inhibitions about self-presentation and self-awareness (Cooper, 1976). This can help a person to a more realistic perception of himself and, possibly, help him to cope better with some of his stresses. This is a method of training that has been criticized because of its potential *stressfulness* for some people (Cooper, 1975); it may seem strange that it is advocated as a means of stress mitigation, but it is another feature of the overall dilemma already mentioned: what may be stressful for one person may be stress relieving for another. Secondly, the course could include training in methods of slowing down the physiological processes, such as yoga or transcendental meditation. No doubt this will be regarded as an absurd suggestion by many management trainers, who would envisage the incredulity and resentment of some course attenders to the suggestion that such techniques could have an appropriate place in management training. Nevertheless, it has been demonstrated that these are methods that succeed in enabling people to relax. For that reason they have a potential place in management training. The third possibility is probably the easiest, and that is to include in a course some focus on or discussion of stress at work. This would at least succeed in bringing the issue out into the open and moderating the degree of shame that course

181

members may feel in acknowledging their own stress proneness.

Operational 4: Lessening Organizational Dependency

If an individual employee is overdependent on his employing organization, there are a number of disadvantages: he is likely to become overcautious, anxious, reluctant and generally view his compliance to the employment contract as being obligatory rather than volitional. Coincidentally, it may make him more susceptible to stress as the anticipated whims and vagaries of superiors assume alarming significance.

In the latter half of the seventies we have a situation of many managers feeling very dependent on their current employer because of the sluggishness of the managerial job market. Other jobs are hard to find and the numbers of the executive jobless continue to rise. Although personnel specialists may not be able to influence the external job market, there are other opportunities to heighten job security by reducing organizational dependence.

One strategy is to give better opportunities for improving professional qualifications. Studies like that of Page (1976) show the relative difficulty of obtaining reemployment among those in executive positions, whose skills and experience have been specific to one organization. When no longer required in that context, a period of retraining is a necessary prerequisite to finding employment elsewhere. Allied to this is the more general problem of skill obsolescence as some specializations become

182

less important in organizational life. Enabling employees to enhance their general employability can increase their sense of job security by increasing the range of options they see before them. It has already been suggested that the purpose of training is to aid the operational performance of those attending courses. If this is achieved by the in-company course, the range of skills and knowledge will be oriented toward those requisite within the organization. Provision of day- and block-release for externally moderated qualifications, like professional-body diplomas and university masters and diploma programs, can provide people with a wider range of enhanced capacities as well as "a piece of paper" with wider currency, avoiding the claustrophobia felt by many executives who see their skills as irrelevant outside their own immediate environment. It is presumably a narrow and outdated view to criticize such opportunities on the grounds that a prized member of the organization is more likely to leave.

A further possibility is to review personnel policy on fringe benefits. It seems particularly pertinent to mention this at a time when there are many rumors, and some evidence, that companies are seeking to extend fringe benefits, like the company car, assisted house purchase, and subsidized lunches; these too can make people organizationally dependent by reducing the freedom of movement of those enjoying the benefits. It would be unrealistic to suggest that such benefits should be removed, but their extension needs very careful consideration.

One of the main determinants of organizational dependency is, of course, the pension arrangement. Most private sector pension schemes provide relatively attractive pensions to the managerial elite but with the penalty of nontransferability or limited transferability.

Operational 4: Clarifying the Criteria for Advancement

The personnel literature is replete with advice on career development and complaints about its scarcity. Glueck (1974) echoes the common cry:

> Unfortunately, most organizations are not at present concerned with career development. They would not think of ignoring financial planning or materials replacement planning, but the human resource is likely to deteriorate or fail to be used well without career development plans.

The proposition that performance is improved if people know what they have to do and how they are getting on may be a way of reducing individual stress. It is anxiomatic that the majority of people in executive positions are seeking advancement to a position of greater authority, scope, or financial remuneration: if this were not so they would not put their foot on the first rung of the ladder. Career development programs that we have seen are usually highly specific for junior positions, with a progressive decline in clarity as the program moves up the hierarchy. The problem is a dual one. First, a program of career development implies that the person who achieves the declared objectives will reap the benefit, and if five people meet the outline requirements to be, for instance, the next marketing manager, only one of them will be successful, and even that depends on the present incumbent deciding to leave or retire. Second, the career development program may be suspect in the face of change; criteria set out in 1977 may have become irrelevant in 1978.

Despite the difficulties, there are usually ways in which the future can be made clearer and more comprehensible for people, and a realistic increase in clarity can help to moderate individual stress.

Operational 5: Self-Analysis Drills

The last of our operational suggestions is a quite original one. Whereas we have so far been considering possible developments in operations already existing in most organizations, this potential initiative is the provision of a self-analysis aid, whereby an individual can carry out his own diagnosis of his own behavior in order to determine whether he is under stress or not. Symptom awareness training is one example of this, and many occupational-health doctors argue that this is the first step in stress prevention. Some company doctors would go further and suggest that this is all that is needed, since the successful management of stress must ultimately rely on the individual's own initiative once he has been made aware of his own stress-related behavior. Not much has been done to implement this type of training in industry, but model programs are available from the mental health field (Noland, 1973).

Influential 1: Industrial Democracy and the Managerial Role

Moving now to our second category, we begin to consider those initiatives related to personnel influence in organizations rather than personnel operations. The first suggestion is concerned with industrial democracy and the role of managers within that type of structure.

Weir (1976) has recently given sharp focus to the widely held belief that managers are apprehensive about the development of union involvement in the management of companies, even when the managers are union members themselves. He surveyed the attitudes of 1,147 managers in a large, profitable organization in the food and drink industry that has a good reputation for employee relations and is regarded as having an overt commitment to progressive personnel policies. Forty-five percent of them felt that they as a category of employees were looked after worse than in the past and that manual workers had more direct and comprehensive access to top management than they had themselves. Later he demonstrates that there is a feeling among his respondents that employees should have a greater say in running the company, but this does not necessarily mean *union* involvement. Forty-seven percent of the union members (14 percent of the sample) were prepared to advocate more involvement by unions in management, but only 17 percent of nonunionists.

The general trend toward industrial democracy is a source of anxiety to managers, producing problems about self-esteem and considerable role ambiguity. Strategies to

186

deal with this are easy to see, but less easy to implement. The obvious initiative is to involve managers in consultation and decision making to the extent they regard as desirable (76 percent of Weir's respondents felt that they were not sufficiently consulted about matters which directly affected them). The obstacles are considerable. First, they are likely to lack the machinery and will to find and accept a common representative figure, because of the diversity of their interests and their concomitant disinterest in unionism. Second, other employees may regard consultation by management with managers as "the opposing high command consulting with the supplies officers before launching the attack." Third, what managers seek from consultation may frequently be the maintenance or extension of a series of differential gaps between themselves and other employees.

The strategy which it is hoped personnel specialists may be able to adopt in this connection is to whittle down the traditional managerial view of status and self-esteem, being seen in terms of hierarchical position and the number of subordinates. If managers can gradually adjust their sights to see their status in terms of contribution to the organization, instead of place in the organization hierarchy, then the stressful potential of industrial democracy and its evolution will be reduced and the potential value of such evolution will itself be enhanced. To achieve such a change will depend on some of the strategies already discussed, such as performance appraisal and training, and will inevitably be influenced by remuneration policy, but the general contribution of personnel specialists to the develop-

187

ment of thinking and employment *policy*, within their companies, is another potential influence.

Influential 2: The Nature of Managerial Jobs

There is a tendency to believe that manual, and some clerical employees, have jobs that are routine and lacking in intrinsic motivations. We need also to realize that some managerial jobs are also of this type. Campbell et al. (1970) surveyed 39 U. S. organizations with a high reputation for the development of managerial talent and concluded:

> Management was characterized by having rather narrow jobs and very tightly written job descriptions that almost seemed designed to take the newness, conflict and challenge out of the job.

The current interest in the quality of working life generally appears to assume that managerial life already has quality and that it is only nonmanagers whose working life needs moderation. The irony is that so many studies and other indicators, like managerial membership of trade unions, indicate a growing disenchantment with many managers failing to find in their work those intrinsic motivations that we are so busily trying to inject into the lives of those engaged in demonstrably prosaic work. The reasons for this are well documented: specialization, technology, organization size, and degree of bureaucratization being the most common, together with resentment of apparent union influence that we have already considered. We should add to this a particular version of the problem of specialization, and that is the growth in the number of specialists, each of whom reduce the wholeness of the job done by someone else. For years this has been seen as the particular problem of the foreman, who has seen his autonomy gradually reduced by the arrival of the work-study specialist, the production controller, the industrial relations officer, etc. More senior managers have not perhaps acknowledged and come to terms with the extent to which the specialists are reducing the wholeness of their jobs too.

Out of the immense and ever expanding literature on motivation and job satisfaction, we can pick the recent work of Hackman and Lawler (1971) who demonstrated the crucial importance of the scope for making a significant contribution to the total task in considering the sources of achievement feelings in individuals at work. Personnel officers should ask themselves to what extent they now are reducing the contribution of other managers, and so removing a key element from the jobs of their managerial colleagues. Influential and well-informed figures (Swannack, 1975; Rogers, 1976) in the personnel management work now aver that those days are past and the reasons are evident: legislation, incomes policy, the need for collective bargaining, the growth of union membership, the decline of employee deference being at the top of the list. The personnel specialist moves to the center of the stage, acquiring the status, power, money, and limelight he has always craved: but his gain is another's loss because the advisory role becomes a control function to achieve consistency, and changes to increase consistency involve reducing discretion and flexibility available to managers. The difficult question here for personnel specialists, in their influencing, is how can managerial jobs gain features to replace the discretion that the specialists remove?

Influential 3: Selection and Promotion Criteria

Change of function within the organization, as well as joining a new one, is a time of stress for the individual. Conventionally, such changes of function are promotions or carry some other benefit to make the change attractive, so there is useful enthusiasm and commitment to counter the stress hazard; however, apart from the normal settling in problems of a new job, there is the question of whether the selection/promotion decision has been soundly based, so that the promotee is being drawn into a new role with which he can cope. The danger is that the Peter Principle will operate and the promotee will find that he has reached the level of his own incompetence and then remain in that stressful situation because he is not able to display sufficient competence to be promoted out of it. The conventional method of avoiding such an error is to exhort the decision makers to pay close attention to the fullness of the job description and to their selection criteria. Equally conventional, however, is the detailed job description and personnel specification that focus on the specialist aspects of the job and guesses about the personal attributes of candidates that will equip them for those specialized tasks. Seldom is this approach effective in telling us what *skills* are called for.

190

A recent advance that may help in improving the effectiveness of job analysis for selection and placement is the important work of Stewart (1976), in attempting to provide generic classifications of management jobs. After analyzing some 450 managerial jobs, she produced a typology based mainly on the nature of the contacts that the job required, as this was regarded as the main differentiation between them. A total of twelve jobs are in four groups: *hub, peer dependent, man management* and *solo*. These terms partly explain themselves, but it is necessary to read the text to see the extent to which this typology succeeds in extending simple common sense ideas about the demands of jobs by drawing in the degree of contacts which job holders have to make inside and outside the organization, the level at which they make internal contacts, the nature of their relationship with the people they contact, the importance of cooperation, the time spent in contact, the significance of bargaining and of risk taking, and other factors which give credence to the typology and thus make it possible to construct job profiles, providing a visual means of comparing the demands of the job a person is in with the demands of a job he might move into.

This provides the opportunity to draw up job descriptions and specifications with an additional dimension relating to the demands of a job, and then shows how the job profile could be used to describe the demands, constraints and choices in a job in such a way that requisite skills can also be described. It would be naive to suggest that this would prevent the promotion of people who are not appropriately qualified. The aspiration of individuals is seldom sufficiently rational for them to accept that a particular promotion would not suit them, in spite of the fact that it pays more than their present position; and those making appointments may not have a field from which to choose. Despite this the Stewart job-profile method might prevent some stressful promotions and would, at least, succeed in describing the demands, constraints, and choices of a new job in enough detail for a promotee to go into a new situation with his eyes open.

Influential 4: Grievance Procedure

There is little evidence recently available on the issues now being processed through grievance channels in organizations, but what is clear is that every employee of an organization, including managers, must be advised of the grievance resolution channel available to him personally. Although this is traditionally the domain of the supervisor taking up the case of an aggrieved manual employee, there is now the possibility of more individuals using this procedure as a way of seeking satisfaction of complaints. We have earlier argued that the main problem of the stressed manager is the difficulty he has in acknowledging that he is under stress in the first place. Therefore, it is not likely that he will make a complaint that he is being stressed, but it may still be useful for the personnel specialist to monitor grievances in procedure as a possible stress indicator. Roethlisberger and Dickson (1939) made the simple and profound observation forty years ago that complaints involving the hopes and fears of employees had both a *manifest* and a *latent* content: saying one thing and meaning rather more. If an organization has managers personally using grievance procedures —which seem unlikely—a pull on that particular communication cord can be a cue to the personnel specialist of a stressful situation. More likely is that grievances coming from other people in the area, for which the manager is responsible, may have a latent content indicating that the manager is showing stress symptoms in his dealings with subordinates.

Influential 5: Managerial Mobility

One very specific source of stress is the need for managers to move to other regions of the country. In certain large companies and public sector organizations this is a well established aspect of personnel policy. Promotion accompanies movement. In this situation the translated manager has the usual problems of a new job plus the domestic and family problems that relocation brings. We suggest that relocation problems are increasing rather than lessening. The direct and indirect financial commitment in buying and selling a house is generally regarded as getting greater, parents frequently feel that the standard of high schools varies so considerably that a geographical move could disadvantage children to a greater extent than when they could move between grammar schools. Most significantly, of all new factors in the mobility argument is the attitude and earning potential of the wife. We do not suggest that all managers are men, but the very great majority of executives are married men. If the wife is content to be a housewife, she has to cope with all the loneliness of settling into a new town

193

while her husband escapes to work with its built-in social contacts. If she is not content with being a housewife, there are a variety of developments which influence her mobility. Twenty percent of households now have the wife as the principal earner. Presumably, few of these are at the earnings level of the conventional mobile manager, but at a time of incomes policy and inflation, the significance of the wife's income is considerable and not to be jeopardized. Also, some of the jobs popular among the wives of mobile managers are less readily transferable than they were. The prime example is schoolteaching, where the numbers of unemployed schoolteachers make it unlikely that a woman can uproot herself from one school and readily find a teaching job at another, even though this was commonplace until recently.

The research of Birch and Macmillan (1971) gives some indication of the scale of managerial mobility. Examining the period up to 1970, they found that an average number of regional moves per manager of 0.7 in 1940 had more than doubled to an average of 1.6 in 1970, with 15 percent of managers moving four or more times in their careers, and university-qualified managers moving more frequently than the average. In addition, in an in-depth study of mobile managers and their wives, Marshall and Cooper (1976a) found that the stresses on the managers and their families during and after a relocation were greater and more complex than anticipated. They concluded that much of the stress and managers' ability to cope depended on the stage of their life cycle (e.g., single, married but no children, married with young children, married with older children, empty nest). Unfortunately, many managers are relocated at the most inappropriate life stage for the family—when the manager has young school-aged children and a "captive wife."

The question we raise here is to ask how necessary is the policy of some organizations in explicitly or implicitly making willingness to move a condition of promotion. Many people will seek geographical relocation at some time in their careers, but if people are not able to determine when and where they move, but have to accept the move when it is offered or slip several prospective rungs on the promotion ladder, then they become candidates for stress because of family-company interface conflict. We believe that the widespread convention of linking promotion with geographical relocation could benefit from reappraisal.

CONCLUSION

There are many other methods and approaches to coping and managing stress, depending on the sources activated and the interface between these sources and the individual make-up of the manager concerned. Nevertheless, one important point that must always be kept in mind in coping with and managing organizational stress is, as Wright (1975b) so aptly summarizes, that "the responsibility for maintaining health should be a reflection of the basic relationship between the individual and the organization for which he works; it is in the best interests of both parties that reasonable steps are taken to live and work sensibly and not too demandingly."

195

8

METHODOLOGICAL PROBLEMS ASSOCIATED WITH STRESS RESEARCH

Psychologists, sociologists and management scientists are only beginning to explore systematically the extent of managerial stress, indeed, occupational stress in general. It is important, therefore, to conclude any assessment of an organizational phenomenon of this sort by examining some of the methodological shortcomings of current research work in the field, to help point the way for future efforts and to forewarn the interested individual of the difficulties of interpretation of the research reported to date.

CONFUSION OF DEPENDENT AND INDEPENDENT VARIABLES

By using the term stress too widely—to denote pressures on the individual (e.g., work load), its effects (e.g., poor work performance), and also his/her reactions (e.g.,

196

depression, escapist drinking, etc.)—researchers have contributed to conceptual and definitional confusion in this area. Weick (1970) emphasizes this point: "It is certainly not a novel observation that the area of stress research has definitional problems. Because stress is so pervasive in human affairs, investigators have been tempted to use expansive definitions that incorporate stimuli, responses, and mediating processes." McGrath (1970b) suggests that we must go beyond merely clarifying the dependent, mediating and independent variables in the stress chain: "We need to approach the problems of stress systematically, with a set of concepts that encompasses the full sequence of events (objective demand, subjective demand, response, and consequences) and with an approach aimed at seeking the linkages among the parts of this sequence." That is, an approach which avoids a simple cause and effect model but rather emphasizes "the use of multiple stress conditions and multiple measures of stress effects." This leads to a second and related problem: how do we analyze research data to provide the most meaningful generalizations, taking into account the full sequence of events?

USE OF CORRELATIONAL ANALYSIS

Most of the stress studies currently being reported (Cooper and Marshall, 1976) rely heavily on the output of simple correlational analysis for their conclusions. There are several serious difficulties with this approach to stress

197

research. First, correlational analysis fails to point out the role of intervening variables. A causal chain is not necessarily only two variables long as many studies would have us believe. Second, even if we took into account a number of possible intervening variables in a multiple correlational design, we would still be unable to determine how much each of the potential stressors, for example, contribute to the manifestation of stress. To do this effectively, we would have to introduce multivariate forms of analysis (e.g., multiple regression analysis), something which has not been done to any large extent in stress research but which is essential for any meaningful work in the future. Third, many of the correlational studies focus on one point in time, which limits the inferences one can draw about causality. More longitudinal data is required, within multivariate designs, to provide more accurate information on the nature and volatility of the stress situation.

MEASUREMENT OF STRESS

Once we have clearly defined the independent (e.g., stressors) and dependent (e.g., emotional and physical ill health) variables, we then have the problem of how to measure them. One difficulty in the field of stress research is that a large number of the studies use *subjective* dependent variables. As Weick (1970) suggests, "despite the fact that stress seems to have a marked effect on behavior, stress researchers have been content to use a surprisingly narrow set of dependent measures. The objection we

198

have is that most of the psychological measures that are used are self-reports." Far too many social science-based research projects in the stress field are using nonobjective measures when they have available to them a number of alternative behavioral and psycho-physiological measures. The advantage of the latter is that they are less open to the problems associated with self-report measures such as acquiescence response set, social desirability effects, and the like. On the other hand, many of the medical researchers in the stress area are using very limited physiological measures (e.g., diastolic blood pressure) without the support of either behavioral or attitudinal measures, the former, although more objective and less amenable to observer or respondent bias, may be less valuable (in isolation) in highlighting the complex phenomenon of individual stress. What is really needed is the cooperation of social scientists and doctors to work together in this field, to share and refine their methodologies, research instruments and perspectives. Without this cooperation work in this area will develop very slowly and may never get to the point of creating meaningful coping and preventative strategies. As McGrath (1970b) emphasizes, "without generalizable methods and measures, the stress research literature will surely fractionate still further—leading to more and more concentration on effort within narrower enclaves, each bounded by a single method, setting, or measure, and unrelated to one another."

There are several other aspects of measurement that are important to consider in stress research. First, that we must attempt to develop measures and precedures which are as unobtrusive (but not deceptive) as possible, so that

199

methodology and research tools don't alter the phenomena to be measured. Second, that some independent variables are susceptible to contamination by the dependent variable being studied. In retrospective studies of coronary heart disease death, for example, occupation (usually taken from the death certificate) may have been directly affected by a preceding illness. Third, it is desirable to do multistressor, multieffect type studies so that we can better understand the complexities of stress situations and coping strategies (McGrath, 1970b).

SAMPLING

There are two different issues we would like to consider in this section. First, how large a sample one should use in stress research. And second, what represents an adequate control group. In response to the first, it seems, from the research work carried out to date, that most research falls in one of two categories: those studies examining in-depth a small, highly specific sample, and those carrying out large-scale research but using simplistic survey techniques. In the former the purpose is to attempt to understand the complexities of this multifaceted problem area using intensive techniques such as interviews, observations, etc. In the latter, the primary concern of the researchers is to be able to generate enough data to be able to generalize from them. Each of these approaches has inherent weaknesses; in the case of the small sample approach, the generalizability of the results are usually limited by the small and selective sample as well as by the sensitivity and social skills of the interviewer/researcher. In the case of the large sample survey technique, one lacks the qualitative data necessary to help untangle the complex interactions implicit in the person : environment fit model of stress elucidated earlier in this book. What is needed, of course, is a combination of both; relatively large scale research which also involves an in-depth study of a smaller, representatively selected sample over time.

In addition to the sample size issue, another methodological concern is the selection of control groups. It is difficult in the stress research area to determine what represents an adequate control group against which to compare stressed managers or any other group. Comparative evaluation of stress requires a well thought out and appropriate comparison or control group. The possible alternatives are (1) normative data on the general population at large, (2) matched sample of the stressed group being studied (on the basis of age, sex, occupational grouping, or any other variable considered relevant), (3) individuals who have *coped* in situations where the stressed have not, (4) individuals suffering from non-stress-related disease. In making decisions about the type of comparison or control group needed, one must make explicit the basis of the research work, that is, the hypotheses one is really testing. There are no hard-and-fast rules about comparative research, but there is a need for researchers to be more honest about their implicit hypotheses, assumptions, and predilections.

RETROSPECTIVE AND PROSPECTIVE STUDIES

Most of the work in stress research has been done retrospectively or at a single point in time. Very little work has been designed on either a long-term basis or prospectively, by collecting data on a representative sample and following that group over time. This means that most of our knowledge is based on correlational-type studies, with all the difficulties this implies, especially the limited capacity to predict causal relationships. Longitudinal research is needed in the future if we are to accurately assess the nature of causality, to unscramble the interrelationships between the individual and environmental stressors, to develop clearer epidemiological pictures of both the stressed and nonstressed, etc.

Nevertheless, current methods do have some strengths; one of the less obvious advantages of latitudinal (one point in time) over longitudinal (over time) studies is that the former can be achieved with the minimum of interference in the individual's (being researched) life. This has both methodological and ethical implications. A major concern of social scientists in any area is that their intervention will have some effect on the mental process, behavior, etc., which they want to study, and that they will not, therefore, obtain a true reading. This is a particularly crucial problem in longitudinal research on stress: the initial contact, whether by questionnaire or interview, is likely to sensitize the individual to the topic and affect his future perception of, coping with, and perhaps even tolerance for, stress. The ultimate outcome for the individual may be either harmful or beneficial; it will, however, almost certainly go beyond the knowledge and the control of the researcher. This is not merely a methodological problem of obtaining distorted results; it is one of the ethics of interfering in individuals' lives. The data-distortion consequences of the alternative one-point-in-time study can be kept to a minimum, but even here the researcher cannot absolve himself from all responsibility for the future consequences of his intervention. In longitudinal research it might be both useful and desirable to combine research with individual counseling. That is, for the researcher to adopt a counseling role, while collecting data by interview, to help the respondent cope with the anxieties generated by the discussion of his/her stress at work or home. This would have not only ethical but also methodological advantages:

1. It would be possible to elicit much franker data by actively involving the respondent in the research process. Researchers would then gain access to the ultimate subjective as well as objective criteria of stress.
2. Data on causes of stress, coping, possible action and their outcomes would all be covered in one research study and on the same population.
3. One would reap the benefits of *known* interventions.

The first advantage is particularly important. In present circumstances a variety of mechanisms appear to be operating to prevent individuals from reporting stress symptoms accurately; chief of these are lack of self-awareness, preference for the socially desirable response, and lack of faith in the confidentiality of research data. Only the development of a long-term, nonthreatening, even supportive, relationship between researcher and respondent can fully justify breaching (even unknowingly) the latters' defenses in any way.

SUGGESTIONS FOR FUTURE RESEARCH

The *individual's* self-awareness, motivations and aspirations (and how these change) are important determinants of his approach to and expectations of work. These not only change with age but also in response to changing conditions in the world outside. The recent economic crisis has had effects on morale and expectations at all levels of the work force and has resulted in even economists recognizing attitudes as respectable variables (e.g., Pickering, Harrison and Cohen, 1973). Researchers must, therefore, look more closely at work attitudes, especially in the area of stress where they play such an important mediating role.

In the context of the *organization,* stress identification studies are only a first step in a more lengthy process of examining the status quo and planning action for its future improvement. By identifying job stresses and satisfaction, we may be able to point to areas of need, but this is no more than a preliminary basis from which remedies can be suggested. Research could also be used to generate ideas as to what actions are appropriate and by whom these should be undertaken. For such a study, the sample needs to be broadened to include company representatives as well as employee managers so that both individual job satisfaction and company performance interests will be adequately represented. If these two sides can, in fact, discuss and negotiate such issues together, solutions to which both are committed can be agreed. Another precondition to effective action is an awareness of (and willingness to change if necessary) company norms and values. These determine individual employees' attitudes to experiencing, revealing and managing stress and currently appear to be acting (not only inside companies but in society as a whole) to deter adaptive coping in certain contexts.

The relationship between *work stress and home life,* in particular, deserves more systematic investigation than it has received. The two most important dimensions, as far as the manager in his work role is concerned, appear to be those of time management and social support. Factors such as the wife's occupation and her satisfaction with this, the part the manager's job plays in their joint life, the extent to which he is required, and wants, to participate in activities outside work, all have significant bearing on these, and ultimately, the manager's performance in his job. Their investigation is of considerable topical interest and should be carried out with continual reference to changes in society's values and practices.

CONCLUSION

McGrath (1970) summarizes the state of stress research aptly when he says "but in whatever subject area and with whatever research approach, the clear and central need is that future research on stress be *systematic* not superficial, *comprehensive* not casual, *programmatic* not piecemeal."

REFERENCES

Appley, M.H., and Trumbull, R. "On the Concept of Psychological Stress," in M.H. Appley and R. Trumbull, *Psychological Stress.* New York: Appleton, 1967.

Argyris, C. *Integrating the Individual and the Organization.* New York: Wiley, 1964.

Arthur, R.J., and Gunderson, E.K. "Promotion and Mental Illness in the Navy," *Journal of Occupational Medicine,* 7 (1965) 452–456.

Bakker, C.D. "Psychological Factors in Angina Pectoris," *Psychosomatic Medicine,* 8 (1967) 43–49.

Bakker, C.D. and Levenson, R.M. Determinants of Angina Pectoris, *Psychosomatic Medicine,* 19 (1967) 621–633.

Barber, R. "Who Would Marry a Director?" *Director,* March (1976) 60–62.

Beattie, R.T., Darlington, T.G., and Cripps, D.M. *The Management Threshold.* BIM Paper OPN 11, 1974.

Bernard, J. "The Eudaemonists," in S.Z. Klausner ed., *Why Man Takes Chances.* New York: Garden City, 1968, pp. 6–47.

Berry, K.J. *Status Integration and Morbidity.* Unpublished Ph.D. thesis (Corvallis: University of Oregon, 1966).

207

Beveridge, W.E. *The Interview in Staff Appraisal.* Allen & Unwin, 1974.

Birch, S., and Macmillan, B. *Managers on the Move: A Study of British Managerial Mobility.* BIM Report No. 7, 1970.

Bortner, R.W., and Rosenman, R.H. "The Measurement of Pattern A Behaviour," *Journal of Chronic Diseases,* 20 (1967) 525–533.

Bowskill, D., and Linacre, A. *The Male Menopause.* Chicago: Muller, 1976.

Brady, J.V. "Ulcers in 'Executive' Monkeys," in R.N. Haber ed., *Current Research in Motivation.* New York: Holt, Rinehart & Winston, 1966, pp. 242–248.

Braine, J. *Life at the Top.* Grinstead, Sussex: Eyre & Straker, 1962.

Breslow, L. and Buell, P. "Mortality from Coronary Heart Disease and Physical Activity of Work in California," *Journal of Chronic Diseases,* 11 (1960) 615–626.

British Institute of Management. *Executive Health Care* (BIM, 1971).

Brook, A. "Mental Stress at Work," *The Practitioner.* 210 (1973) 500–508.

Brooks, G.W., and Mueller, E.F. "Serum Urate Concentrations Among University Professors," *Journal of the American Medical Association,* 195 (1966) 415–418.

Brozek, J., Keys A., and Blackburn, H. "Personality Differences Between Potential Coronary and Non-Coronary Patients," *Annals of New York Academy of Science,* 134 (1966) 1057–1064.

Bruhn, J.G., Chandler, B. and Wolf, S. "A Psychological Study of Survivors and Non-Survivors of Myocardial Infarction," *Psychosomatic Medicine,* 31 (1969) 8–19.

Buck, V. *Working Under Pressure.* London: Staples Press, 1972.

Budner, S. "Intolerance of Ambiguity as a Personality Variable," *Journal of Personality,* 30 (1962).

Burns, L.E. *Management of Stress*, A one week residential course organized by the University of Manchester, Extra-Mural Dept. July (1976).

Campbell, J., Lawler, E.E., Dunett, M., and Weick, K.E. *Managerial Behaviour, Performance and Effectiveness.* McGraw Hill, 1970.

Cannon, W.B. "Stresses and Strains of Homeostasis," *American Journal of Medical Science,* 189, 1 (1935).

Caplan, R.D., Cobb, S., and French, J.R.P. "Relationships of Cessation of Smoking with Job Stress, Personality and Social Support," *Journal of Applied Psychology,* 60, 2 (1975) 211–219.

Caplan, R.D., Cobb, S., French, J.R.P., Van Harrison, R., and Pinneau, S.R. *Job Demands and Worker Health: Main Effects and Occupational Differences.* Niosh Research Report, 1975.

Caplan, R.D., and Jones, K.W. "Effects of Workload, Role Ambiguity and Type-A Personality on Anxiety, Depression and Heart Rate," *Journal of Applied Psychology,* 60, 6 (1975) 713–719.

Coch, L., and French, J.R.P. "Overcoming Resistance to Change," *Human Relations,* 11 (1948) 512–532.

Conley, R.W., Conwell, M., and Arill, M.B. "An Approach to Measuring the Cost of Mental Illness," in R.L. Noland ed., *Industrial Mental Health and Employee Counselling.* New York: Behavioural Publications, 1973.

Constandse, W.J. "Mid-40's Man: A Neglected Personnel Problem," *Personnel Journal,* 51, 2 (1972) 129.

Cooper, C.L. *Developing Social Skills in Managers.* Macmillan, 1976.

———. *Group Training for Individual and Organizational Development.* Basel, Switzerland: S. Karger, 1973.

———. How Psychologically Dangerous Are T-Groups and Encounter Groups?" *Human Relations,* 28, 3 (1975) 248–261.

Cooper, C.L., and Marshall, J. "The Management of Stress," *Personnel Review,* 4,4 (1975).

————. "Occupational Sources of Stress: A Review of the Literature Relating to Coronary Heart Disease and Mental Ill Health," *Journal of Occupational Psychology,* 49 (1976) 11–28.

————. "The Changing Roles of British Executives' Wives," *Management International Review.*

Davis, L. "Face the Future with Skill and Enthusiasm," *The Times,* 6th March (1975).

De Bono, E. *Lateral Thinking: A Textbook of Creativity.* London: Wood Lock, 1970.

Dohrenwend, B.S., and Dohrenwend, B.P. *Stressful Life Events.* New York: Wiley 1974.

Donaldson, J., and Gowler, D. "Perogatives, Participation and Managerial Stress," in D. Gowler and K. Legge eds., *Managerial Stress.* Epping: Gower Press, 1975.

Doyle, C. "Stress Isn't Such a Killer After All," *Observer,* 9th November (1975).

Dreyfuss, F., and Czackes, J.W. "Blood Cholesterol and Uric Acid of Health Medical Students Under Stress of Examination," *Archives of International Medicine,* 103 (1959) 798.

Eaton, M.T. "The Mental Health of the Older Executive," *Geriatrics,* 24 (1969) 126–134.

Erikson, J., Edwards, D., and Gunderson, E.K. "Status Congruency and Mental Health," *Psychological Reports,* 33 (1973) 395–401.

Erikson, J., Pugh, W.M., and Gunderson, E.K. "Status Congruency as a Predictor of Job Satisfaction and Life Stress," *Journal of Applied Psychology,* 56 (1972) 523–525.

Eysenck, H.J., Arnold, W.J., and Meili, R. eds., *Encyclopedia of Psychology.* Bungay, Suffolk: Richard Clay (The Chaucer Press) Ltd., 1972.

Farid, S.M. *The Current Tempo of Fertility in England and Wales.* London: HMSO, 1974.

Finn, F., Hickey, N., and O'Doherty, E.F. "The Psychological Profiles of Male and Female Patients with CHD," *Irish Journal of Medical Science,* 2 (1969) 339–341.

Forster, E.M. "Sayings of the Week," *The Observer,* October 6th (1951).

French, J.R.P. "Person-Role Fit," *Occupational Mental Health,* 3, 1 (1973).

French, J.R.P., and Caplan, R.D. "Organizational Stress and Individual Strain," in Marrow ed. *The Failure of Success.* New York: Amacon, 1973, pp. 30–66.

———. "Psychosocial Factors in Coronary Heart Disease," *Industrial Medicine.* 39 (1970) 383–397.

French, J.R.P., Israel, J., and As, D. "An Experiment in Participation in a Norwegian Factory," *Human Relations,* 13,1 (1960) 3–20.

French, J.R.P., Tupper, C.J., and Mueller, E.I. *Workload of University Professors.* Unpublished research report (Ann Arbor, Mich: University of Michigan, 1965).

Fried, M. "Transitional Functions of Working Class Communities: Implications for Forced Relocation," in M.B. Kantor ed., *Mobility and Mental Health.* Conference on Community Mental Health Research, Fifth Washington University Social Science Institute Conference (St. Louis: Thomas, 1965).

Friedman, M. *Pathogenesis of Coronary Artery Disease.* New York: McGraw Hill, 1969.

Friedman, M., Rosenman, R.H., and Carroll, V. "Changes in Serum Cholesterol and Blood Clotting Time in Men Subjected to Cyclic Variations of Occupational Stress," *Circulation,* 17 (1958) 852–861.

Froberg, J., Karlsson, C.G., Levi, L., and Lidberg, L. "Physiological and Biochemical Stress Reactions Induced by Psychosocial Stimuli," in L. Levi ed., *Society, Stress and Disease,* Vol. 1. London: Oxford University Press, 1971 pp. 280–298.

Gemill, G.R., and Heisler, W.J. "Machiavellianism as a Factor in Managerial Job Strain, Job Satisfaction and Upward Mobility," *Academy of Management Journal,* 15, 1 (1972) 51–62.

Gillespie, F. "Stress Costs More Than Strikes," *Financial Times,* 26th April (1974).

Glueck, W.F. *Personnel: A Diagnostic Approach.* Irwin-Dorsey, 1974.

Goffman, E. "On Cooling the Mark Out," *Psychiatry,* 15, 4 (1952) 451–63.

Golembiewski, B.T., and McConkie, M. "The Centrality of Interpersonal Trust," in C.L. Cooper ed., *Theories of Group Processes.* New York: Wiley, 1975.

Gowler, D., and Legge, K. "Stress and External Relationships— the 'Hidden Contract,' " in D. Gowler and K. Legge eds., *Managerial Stress.* Epping: Gower Press, 1975.

Guardian, The. Finniston Slams D.O.I. Delay Over Shotton, 15th April (1976) 20.

Guest, D., and Williams, R. "How Home Affects Work," *New Society,* 18th January (1973).

Gurin, G., Veroff, J., and Feld, S. *Americans View Their Mental Health.* New York: Basic Books, 1960.

Hackman, J.R., and Lawler, E.E. "Employee Reactions to Job Characteristics," *Journal of Applied Psychology,* 55 (1971).

Hamburg, A., and Adams, H. "Seeking and Using Information in Major Transitions," *Archives of General Psychiatry,* 17 (1967) 277–284.

Handy, C. "Difficulties of Combining Family and Career," *The Times,* 22nd September (1975) 16.

Hartston, W.R., and Mottram, R.D. *Personality Profiles of Managers: A Study of Occupational Differences.* Cambridge: ITRU Publication SL9, 1975.

Havighurst, R.J., Munnichs, J.M.A., Neugarten, B., and Thomas, H. eds. *Adjustment to Retirement: A Cross National Sample.* Assen, The Netherlands: Van Gorcum Ltd. 1969.

Heller, J. *Something Happened.* New York: Ballantine Books, 1975.

Herzberg, F. *Work and the Nature of Man.* London: Staples Press, 1966.

Hinkle, L.E. "The Concept of 'Stress' in the Biological and Social Sciences," *Science, Medicine and Man,* 1 (1973) 31–48.

Holmes, T.H., and Masuda, M. "Life Change and Illness Susceptibility," *Separation and Depression AAAS,* (1973) 161–186.

Howells, R., and Barrett, B. *The Health and Safety at Work Act: A Guide for Managers.* London: Institute of Personnel Management, 1975.

Immundo, L.V. "Problems Associated with Managerial Mobility," *Personnel Journal,* 53, 12 (1974) 910.

Jackson, E.F. "Status Consistency and Symptoms of Stress," *American Sociological Review,* 27, 4 (1962) 469–480.

Jenkins, C.D. "Psychologic and Social Precursors of Coronary Disease," *New England Journal of Medicine,* 284, 5 (1971a) 244–255, 6 (1971b) 307–17.

Johnson, A.G. "The Manager—Employer or Employee?" *Personnel Management,* 8, 11 (1976) 20–23.

Kahn, R.L. "Conflict, Ambiguity and Overload: Three Elements in Job Stress," *Occupational Mental Health,* 3,1 (1973).

———. "Some Propositions Toward a Researchable Conceptualization of Stress," in J.E. McGrath ed., *Social and Psychological Factors in Stress.* New York: Holt, Rinehart & Winston, 1970, pp. 97–103.

Kahn, R.L., Wolfe, D.M., Quinn, R.P., Snoek, J.E., and Rosenthal, R.A. *Organizational Stress.* New York: Wiley, 1964.

Kasl, S.V. "Mental Health and the Work Environment," *Journal of Occupational Medicine,* 15, 6 (1973) 509–518.

Kasl, S., and Cobb, S. "Effects of Parental Status Incongruence and Discrepancy in Physical and Mental Health of Adult Offspring," *Journal of Personality and Social Psychology,* Monograph 7, Whole No. 642 (1967) 1–15.

Kay, E. "Middle Management," in J. O'Toole ed., *Work and the Quality of Life.* Cambridge, Mass: MIT Press, 1974.

Kearns, J.L. *Stress in Industry.* London: Priory Press, 1973.

Kecka, W.R., Nie, N.H., and Hull, C.H. *Statistical Package*

213

for the Social Sciences Primer. New York: McGraw Hill, 1975.

Kornhauser, A. *Mental Health of the Industrial Worker.* New York: Wiley, 1965.

Kreitman, N. "Married Couples Admitted to Mental Hospital," *British Journal of Psychiatry,* 114 (1968) 699–718.

Kritsikis, S.P., Heinemann, A.L., and Eitner, S. "Die Angina Pectoris im Aspeckt Ihrer Korrelation mit Biologischer Disposition, Psychologischen und Soziologischem Emflussfaktoren," *Deutsch Gasundh,* 23 (1968) 1878–1885.

Laing, R.D., Ronald, D., and Esterton, A. *Sanity Madness and the Family.* London: Tavistock Publications Ltd., 1964.

Lazarus, R.S. "Cognitive and Personality Factors Underlying Threat and Coping," in M.H. Appley and R. Trumbull eds., *Psychological Stress.* New York: Appleton, 1967.

————. "The Concepts of Stress and Disease," in L. Levi ed., *Society, Stress and Disease,* vol. 1. London: Oxford University Press, 1971, pp. 53–60.

————. *Psychological Stress and the Coping Process.* New York: McGraw Hill, 1966.

Lebovits, B.Z., Shekelle, R.B., and Ostfeld, A.M. "Prospective and Retrospective Studies of CHD," *Psychosomatic Medicine,* 19 (1967) 265–272.

Leighton, D.C., Harding, J.S., Macklin, D.B., Macmillan, A.M., and Leighton, A.H. *The Character of Danger.* New York: Basic Books, 1963.

Levinson, H. "Problems that Worry our Executives," in A.J. Marrow ed., *The Failure of Success.* New York: Amacon, 1973.

Levy, R. "Relief of the Executive Headache?" *Duns,* 10th March (1973) 101.

Lipawski, Z.J. "Psychosocial Aspects of Disease," *Annals of International Medicine,* 71 (1969) 1197–2006.

Love, A.E.H. *The Mathematical Theory of Elasticity.* New York: Dover Publications, 1944, pp. 7–14.

Luce, G.G. *Body Time.* St. Albans, Herts: Paladin, 1973.

214

McGrath, J.E. "A Conceptual Formulation for Research on Stress," in J.E. McGrath ed., *Social and Psychological Factors in Stress.* New York: Holt, Rinehart & Winston, 1970b, pp. 10–21.

———. "Major Substantive Issues: Time, Setting and the Coping Process," in J.E. McGrath ed., *Social and Psychological Factors in Stress.* New York: Holt, Rinehart & Winston, 1970c, pp. 22–40.

——— ed. *Social and Psychological Factors in Stress.* New York: Holt, Rinehart & Winston, 1970a.

Maclean, A. "Emerging Trends in Industrial Mental Health Programmes," in R.L. Noland ed., *Industrial Mental Health and Employee Counselling.* New York: Behavioural Publications, 1973.

McLean, A.A. "Job Stress and the Psychosocial Pressures of Change," *Personnel,* Jan-Feb (1976).

McMurray, R.N. "The Executive Neurosis," in R.L. Noland ed., *Industrial Mental Health and Employee Counselling.* New York: Behavioural Publications, 1973b.

———. "Mental Illness: Society's and Industry's Six Billion Dollar Burden," in R.L. Noland ed., *Industrial Mental Health and Employee Counselling.* New York: Behavioural Publications, 1973a.

Manchester, Conference on *Stresses of the Air Traffic Control Officer (Latest Developments)* (1976).

Marcson, S. *Automation, Alienation and Anomie.* New York: Harper & Row, 1970.

Margolis, B.L., and Kroes, W.H. "Work and the Health of Man," in J. O'Toole ed., *Work and the Quality of Life.* Cambridge, Mass: MIT Press, 1974.

Margolis, B.L., Kroes, W.H., and Quinn, R.P. "Job Stress: An Unlisted Occupational Hazard," *Journal of Occupational Medicine,* 16, 10 (1974) 654–661.

Marrow, A.J. "The Failure of Success," in A.J. Marrow ed., *The Failure of Success.* New York: Amacon, 1973.

Marshall, J. *Job Pressures and Satisfactions at Managerial Lev-*

els. Unpublished doctoral thesis (University of Manchester, 1977).

Marshall, J., and Cooper, C.L. "Managerial Mobility," in D. Ashton ed., *Management Bibliographies and Reviews,* vol 2. Bradford: MCB Ltd. 1976b.

————. *The Mobile Manager and His Wife.* MCB Monograph, first appeared as Management Decision, 14, 4 (1976a) 1–48.

Maxwell, V.B. "Environmental Factors Affecting the Controller," paper presented to conference on *Stresses of the Air Traffic Control Officer (Latest Developments),* (Manchester, 1976).

Mettlin, C., and Woelfel, J. "Interpersonal Influence and Symptoms of Stress," *Journal of Health and Social Behaviour,* 15, 4 (1974) 311–319.

Miller, A. *Death of a Salesman.* New York: Viking, 1964.

Miller, J.G. "Information Input Overload and Psychopathology," *American Journal of Psychiatry,* 8 (1969) 116.

Mills, I.H. "The Disease of Failure of Coping," *The Practitioner,* 217 (1976) 529–538.

Minzberg, H. *The Nature of Managerial Work.* New York: Harper & Row, 1973.

Morokoff, A.M., and Rand, M.A. "Personality and Adaptation to Coronary Artery Disease," *Journal of Consulting Clinical Psychology,* 32 (1968) 648–653.

Morris, J. "Managerial Stress and 'The Cross of Relationships,' " in D. Gowler and K. Legge eds., *Managerial Stress.* Epping: Gower Press, 1975.

Morris, J.N. *et al.* Coronary Heart Disease and Physical Activity of Work, II Statement and Testing of Provisional Hypothesis," *The Lancet,* 2 (1953) 1111–1120.

Neff, W.S. *Work and Human Behaviour.* New York: Atherton Press, 1968.

Nichols, P. *Forget-Me-Not Lane.* London: Faber, 1971.

Nobbs, D. *The Fall and Rise of Reginald Perrin.* Harmondsworth, Middx: Penguin Books, 1976.

Noland, R.L. *Industrial Mental Health and Employee Counsell-ing.* New York: Behavioural Publications, 1973.

Orwell, G. *Nineteen Eighty-Four.* London: Secker & Warburg, 1949.

Osler, W. "The Lumleian Lectures on Angina Pectoris," *The Lancet,* 1 (1910) 696–700, 839–844, 974–977.

Ostfeld, A.M., Lebovits, B.Z., and Shekelle, R.B. "A Prospective Study of the Relationship Between Personality and CHD," *Journal of Chronic Diseases,* 17 (1964) 265–276.

O'Toole, J. *Work and the Quality of Life.* Cambridge, Mass: MIT Press, 1974.

Owen, L. "Bureaucratic vs Entrepreneurial Husbands," *The Guardian,* 24th September (1976).

Packard, V. *A Nation of Strangers.* New York: McKay, 1975.

Paffenbarger, R.S., Wolf, P.A., and Notkin, J. "Chronic Disease in Former College Students," *American Journal of Epidemiology,* 83 (1966) 314–328.

Page, N. "Executive Unemployment and Personal Redundancy," *Personnel Review,* 5,2 (1976).

Pahl, J.M., and Pahl, R.E. *Managers and their Wives.* London: Allen Lane, 1971.

Parkes, C. Murray. "Psycho-Social Transitions," *Social Science and Medicine,* 5 (1971) 101–115.

Parkinson, C.N. *Parkinson's Law.* London: John Murray, 1975.

Parsons, T. "The Kinship System of the Contemporary United States," *American Anthropology,* 45 (1943) 22–38.

Payne, R. " 'A' Type Work for 'A' Type People?" *Personnel Management,* 7 (1975) 22–24.

Pickering, J.F., Harrison, J.A., and Cohen, C.D. "Identification and Measurement of Consumer Confidence: Methodology and Some Preliminary Results," *Journal of the Royal Statistical Society,* 136, 1 (1973) 43–63.

Pierson, G.W. *The Moving American.* New York: Knopf, 1972.

Pincherle, G. *Fitness for Work.* Proceedings of the Royal Society of Medicine, 65, 4 (1972) 321–324.

Porter, L.W., and Lawler, E.E. "Properties of Organization

217

Structure in Relation to Job Attitudes and Job Behaviour," *Psychological Bulletin,* 64 (1965) 23–51.

Prentice, G. "Faith at Work: The Message Is the Mission," *Personnel Management,* 8, 3 (1976).

Quinlan, C.B., Burrow, J.G., and Hayes, C.G. "The Association of Risk Factors and CHD in Trappist and Benedictine Monks," Paper presented to the *American Heart Association,* New Orleans, Louisiana (1969).

Quinn, R.P., Seashore, S., and Mangione, I. *Survey of Working Conditions.* U.S. Government Printing Office, 1971.

Randell, G.A. *et al. Staff Appraisal.* Institute of Personnel Management, 1972.

Rapoport, R., and Rapoport, R.N. *Dual-Career Families Re-Examined.* London: Martin Robertson, 1976.

––––––. "New Light on the Honeymoon," *Human Relations,* 17 (1964).

Roethlisberger, F.J., and Dickson, W.J. *Management and the Worker.* Harvard, 1939.

Rogers, T.G.P. "Personnel Moves Centre Stage," *Personnel Management,* 8, 10 (1976).

Rosenman, R.H., Friedman, M., and Jenkins, C.D. "Clinically Unrecognized Myocardial Infarction in the Western Collaborative Group Study," *American Journal of Cardiology,* 19 (1967) 776–782.

Rosenman, R.H., Friedman, M., and Strauss, R. "CHD in the Western Collaborative Group Study," *Journal of the American Medical Association,* 195 (1966) 86–92.

––––––. "A Predictive Study of CHD," *Journal of the American Medical Association,* 189 (1964) 15–22.

Russek, H.I., and Zohman, B.L. "Relative Significance of Hereditary, Diet and Occupational Stress in CHD of Young Adults," *American Journal of Medical Science,* 235 (1958) 266–275.

Sales, S.M. *Differences Among Individuals in Affective, Behavioural, Biochemical and Physiological Responses to Variations in Work Load.* Doctoral Dissertation, The University of Michigan (Ann Arbor, Mich: University Microfilms, No. 60–18098, 1968).

Sartre, J.P. *Huis Clos.* Paris: Theatre Gallimard, 1947.

Seidenberg, R. *Corporate Wives—Corporate Casualties.* American Management, 1973.

Selye, H. "The General Adaptation Syndrome and the Diseases of Adaptation," *Journal of Clinical Endocrinology,* 6, 117 (1946).

Shekelle, R.G., Ostfeld, A.M., and Paul, O. "Social Status and Incidence of CHD," *Journal of Diseases,* 22 (1969) 381–394.

Shepard, J.M. *Automation and Alienation.* Cambridge, Mass: MIT Press, 1971.

Shirom, A., Eden, D., Silberwasser, S., and Kellerman, J.J. "Job Stresses and Risk Factors in Coronary Heart Disease Among Occupational Categories in Kibbutzim," *Social Science and Medicine,* 7 (1973) 875–892.

Sleeper, R.D. "Labour Mobility Over the Life Cycle," *British Journal of Industrial Relations,* XIII, 2 (1975).

Sofer, C. *Men in Mid-Career.* Cambridge University Press, 1970.

Stewart, R. *Contrasts in Management.* McGraw Hill, 1976.

Swannack, A.R. "Laying a Ghost to Rest," *Personnel Management,* 7, 12 (1975).

Taylor, G.R. *Rethink.* London: Secker and Warburg, 1972.

Taylor, R. "Stress at Work," *New Society,* October 17th (1974).

Terhure, W.B. "Emotional Problems of Executives in Time," *Industrial Medical Surgery,* 32 (1963) 1–67.

Thomas, C.B., and Ross, D.C. Observations of Some Possible Precursors of Essential Hypertension and Coronary Heart Disease in Social Stress and Cardiovascular Disease, *Millbank Memorial Fund Qtrly,* XLV, 2 (1967).

Times, The. Reference to Middle Class Housing Estate Study by Dr. E.G. Cohen, Civil Service College, 29th August (1975).

Toffler, A. *Future Shock.* New York: Random House, 1970.

Torrington, D., and Cooper, C.L. "The Management of Stress and the Personnel Initiative," *Personnel Review* (1977).

Uris, A. "How Managers Ease Job Pressures," *International Management,* 27th June (1972) 45–46.

Van Harrison, R. "Job Stress and Worker Health: Person-Environment Misfit." Paper presented at the *103rd Annual Meeting of the American Public Health Association* (Chicago, Illinois, 1975).

Vickers, R. "A Short Measure of the Type A Personality," *ISR Newsletter,* Michigan, February (1973).

Wagstaff, A.E. "The Dilemma of the Middle-Aged Controller." Paper presented to the conference *Stresses of the Air Traffic Control Officer (Latest Developments)* (Manchester, April 1976).

Wan, T. "Status Stress and Morbidity: A Sociological Investigation of Selected Categories of Work-Limiting Chronic Conditions," *Journal of Chronic Diseases,* 24 (1971) 453–468.

Wardwell, W.I., Hyman, M., and Bahnson, C.B. "Stress and Coronary Disease in Three Field Studies," *Journal of Chronic Diseases,* 17 (1964) 73–84.

Weick, K.E. "The 'Ess' in Stress: Some Conceptual and Methodological Problems," in J.E. McGrath ed., *Social and Psychological Factors in* Stress. New York: Holt, Rinehart & Winston, 1970, pp. 287–347.

Weir, D. "Radical Managerialism: Middle Managers' Perceptions of Collective Bargaining," *British Journal of Industrial Relations,* XIV, 3 (1976).

Wells, W., and Gubar, G. "Life Style Concept in Marketing Research," *Journal of Marketing,* 31, 4 (1966).

Wilson, S. *The Man in the Grey Flannel Suit.* New York: Rentloy (reprint), 1973.

Wind, Y. "A Reward-Balance Model of Buying Behaviour," in G. Fisk ed., *New Essays in Marketing Theory.* Boston,: Allyn and Bacon Inc, 1971.

Wolff, H.G., and Goodell, H. *Stress and Disease,* 2nd ed. Springfield, Illinois: C.C. Thomas, 1968.

References

Wright, H.B. *Executive Ease and Disease.* Epping: Gower Press, 1975b.

_____. "Health Hazards for Executives," *Journal of General Management,* 2, 2(1975a).

_____. "Institute of Directors Medical Centre in London," in A.A. McLean ed., *To Work is Human: Mental Health and the Business Community.* New York: Rand, 1967.

Whyte, W.H. *Patterns for Industrial Peace.* New York: Harper & Row, 1951.

Zyzanski, S.J., and Jenkins, C.D. "Basic Dimension Within the Coronary-Prone Behaviour Pattern," *Journal of Chronic Diseases,* 22 (1970) 781–795.

221

INDEX

223

Index